EVEN GOD WOULD COMPLAIN IN THE UNITED STATES

A French Odyssey in The American Dream

Guy Blaise

COPYRIGHT PAGE

EVEN GOD WOULD COMPLAIN IN THE UNITED STATES : A French Odyssey in The American Dream

Copyright © 2023 by Guy Blaise

DEDICATION

To my beloved children, you are the stars that illuminate the pages of my life. In your laughter, I find the melody of joy, and in your journey, I discover the profound chapters of love. This book is dedicated to you, my eternal source of inspiration and the embodiment of my deepest hopes and dreams.

TABLE OF CONTENT

INTRODUCTION

EVEN GOD WOULD COMPLAIN IN THE UNITED STATES : A French Odyssey in The American Dream

"On ne peut pas aimer la pomme et détester le pommier."

(You can't love apples and hate apple trees.)

Greetings, my dear friends! Bonjour to all of you! I am Guy Blaise, an intrepid immigrant who journeyed from the heart of France to the land of the stars and stripes—the United States. As I bid farewell to my beloved France, I carried with me a deep conviction that the United States was, without a doubt, one of the finest countries to call home.

In the beginning, my perceptions of America were shaped by the negative images disseminated by French television channels. However, I soon discovered that these portrayals were often exaggerated caricatures. Culturally, I was convinced that the U.S. stood out as a captivating tapestry of diversity.

My decision to embark on this American adventure was fueled by an insatiable curiosity that had gripped me since my earliest years. From a tender age, I had been captivated by this land of musical maestros, athletic juggernauts, and the legendary elixir known as Coca-Cola.

One fateful day, while gazing upon the towering figure of Lady Liberty, I had an epiphany: why not share my adventures and musings with all of you fine folks? And so, I resolved to unveil my diary, a chronicle that begins from the very moment I set foot in the land of the free, where freedom and fascination intersect.

From the bewildering world of mass shootings to the head-spinning realm of politics, my tales are many. My diary is a humble immigrant's perspective on the daily reverberations that ripple through this great nation. It is peppered with anecdotes that will evoke laughter and perhaps leave you scratching your head. After all, the United States of America—you can love it, you can like it, but perfection? Well, my friends, that is not precisely its strong suit!

In the U.S., you will find an abundance of wonderful and fascinating people and sites. It is far from being a dreadful country; quite the opposite, it is often considered among the world's best. The unwavering self-assuredness of Americans, deeply ingrained from birth, stems from the belief that there is no superior nation on Earth. This is a cultural phenomenon, born from the idea that Americans were pioneers in modern times for rejecting monarchy, and this perception of uniqueness still endures.

The 4th of July, a day when you witness a sea of flags and an assortment of revelers, serves as a vivid example of American exuberance. It encompasses a diverse array of individuals, from fervent patriots to boisterous personalities.

A considerable segment of the American populace maintains the belief that their military has not suffered defeat in recent history and attributes any "lost wars" to voluntary withdrawals rather than military failures. This sentiment underscores the enduring pride and self-confidence that pervades American society.

May God bless the United States of America as we embark on this journey together!

CHAPTER 1

FROM PARIS TO PERPLEXITY: AN ENCOUNTER WITH THE AMERICAN DREAM

*"Quand le rêve est trop long, le réveil est brutal." - **Ninho***

(When the dream is too long, the awakening is brutal.)

The American dream was sold to me during my student days in Paris. I was brimming with aspirations, much like the grandeur of a cathedral, and my dreams were firmly set on making it to America, the world's wealthiest nation.

Upon my arrival, I was resolute in my pursuit of success. However, I soon found myself unprepared for the American lifestyle and the culture of consumerism.

At my job, I mirrored the typical American routine: hopping into my car, going out for lunch, grabbing a meal, and returning to work. But living like an American comes at a cost, especially when it comes to dining out. It wasn't long before an Ethiopian friend and colleague stopped me on my way back from lunch and posed a thought-provoking question: "Why do you dine out? You can't live like Americans; their minds are wired for excessive spending."

In my eagerness to assimilate into American life, I made a grave error. The trouble began when my bank offered me a credit card. I mistakenly believed it was a gesture of goodwill from my bank due to my loyal patronage. Little did I know that by repaying only the minimum amount each month, the bank would profit from the accumulating interest. Over five years, I toiled to pay off a $1,000 credit card debt and realized that credit cards are like mischievous imps lurking in your pocket—tempting, easily swappable, and perpetually dangling the carrot of repayment. It's a sly trap; every time I exceeded my limit, an overdraft awaited me. To regain control of my finances, I transitioned to using cash and adjusted my spending habits.

At my workplace, I noticed that it was primarily immigrants who brought homemade meals to the cafeteria, while most Americans chose to dine out. This culture of constantly having a backup plan in case the preceding one fails is exhausting. It's easy to accumulate unnecessary items, often obtained on credit. Without financial prudence, debt lurks around every corner.

Despite my initial American optimism that tomorrow would be better, I converted my salary and compared it to what I would earn in France. In monetary terms, I was better off in the U.S., yet the stark reality was somewhat different. I sold my apartment and purchased a house, as I was advised by many that renting equated to money down the drain. The house, a charming three-bedroom with a balcony, made me eager to welcome visitors from France. When my brother and his wife arrived, their immediate impression was that I was living in a grand mansion.

However, I soon realized that Americans are drawn to larger houses as a symbol of social success, but it comes with a myriad of responsibilities. Homeownership translates to maintenance, utility payments, property taxes, and insurance on top of the mortgage. Many of my American friends owned at least two cars, and that meant paying insurance for both vehicles.

My Ethiopian friend's advice echoed in my mind. I needed to ground myself and prioritize the essentials; otherwise, my American dream would soon become a nightmare. Some of my friends came from well-off families, so money was not a concern. However, there were also those who lived beyond their means, much like the majority of Americans.

Regarding health, I was in good shape, though I became more discerning about fast food and American cuisine. Despite having health coverage through my job, I couldn't help but feel a sense of insecurity. The thought of healthcare in Canada crossed my mind as a backup plan because healthcare costs in the U.S. can easily lead to bankruptcy.

And then there were the relentless waves of advertising, holiday sales, and the infamous Black Friday. Black Friday, the day after Thanksgiving, happens to be my least favorite time of the year. Americans are enticed into creating artificial needs through sales, resulting in shopping cart collisions and even fatalities over an iPad or television. It's a disturbing form of human alienation. As time passed, I adopted a more philosophical perspective, observing this unquenchable thirst for more, all while our planet teetered on the brink of danger. It seemed a profound irresponsibility.

As America exports its "culture," even France embraced Black Friday, albeit with a sense of French irony. Personally, for this year's Black Friday, I will be purchasing a bottle of wine, some cheese, and a baguette—embracing the simple pleasures.

CHAPTER 2

THE AMERICAN LOVE AFFAIR: ICE, KETCHUP, AND A CHAOTIC DINNER DANCE

"Il faut manger pour vivre et non pas vivre pour manger." **Moliere**

(You must eat to live and not live to eat.)

The American approach to food and meals never ceases to amaze me. It's an unstructured affair where the notion of three square meals a day often falls by the wayside. Americans snack whenever hunger strikes, irrespective of the clock.

What truly baffles me is their habit of dining at 5 pm. Observing an American at a meal feels like they're in a race against time: food vanishes from their plates with lightning speed, and the contents of their dishes often leave me perplexed. I often find myself wishing I could decipher the intricate mysteries of American taste buds.

Some days, I am left wondering why Americans pile everything onto one plate, casting only a casual glance toward the vegetables, sometimes even squeezing dessert amidst the savory chaos. It frequently appears that vegetables hold a higher value than meat in the U.S. This leads me to question how one can truly savor a meal and appreciate the culinary artistry when everything is mingled on a single plate.

Another cultural shock that intrigues me is the practice of unlimited soda refills in restaurants. One of the most amusing restaurant quirks, in my opinion, involves serving drinks—from Coca-Cola to cocktails—with more ice cubes than actual beverage. And then there's the ubiquitous penchant for deep-frying almost anything and generously slathering ketchup on nearly everything.

I recall my first Christmas party dinner at my workplace, where my colleagues at the table were dousing their plates with ketchup like kindergarteners. I was amazed by their unusual taste, feeling as if I had witnessed a culinary extravaganza. It was also my first encounter with green ketchup—oh la la!

When Americans are asked about their affinity for ketchup, they often point to the use of "fresh tomato and water," but tend to overlook that American ketchup, like Heinz, is laden with sugar.

Undoubtedly, the United States is a relatively young country compared to France, and I've noticed that Americans lack a deeply ingrained culinary culture. It sometimes feels like all everyone knows is mac and cheese. God save America!

CHAPTER 3

MCDONALD'S: AMERICA'S UNOFFICIAL CUISINE, WHERE CONVENIENCE MEETS CULINARY QUIRKS

"Le secret pour bien vivre et longtemps est: manger la moitie, marcher le double, rire le triple et aimer sans mesure." **French saying**

(The secret to living well and long is: eat half, walk double, laugh triple, and love without measure.)

In the United States, there exists a pervasive perception that McDonald's qualifies as real food. While many acknowledge its lack of nutritional value, it maintains its popularity owing to its convenience, appealing taste, and affordability. Healthy food options are often viewed as expensive, while less nutritious alternatives are readily available at lower costs.

The United States does not possess a single, unified cuisine but rather a myriad of culinary traditions deeply rooted in the diversity of its states. Despite this rich culinary heritage, a significant number of Americans have embraced a lifestyle of dining out instead of cooking at home. They frequent a spectrum of establishments, from high-end restaurants to fast-food joints, savoring favorites such as pizza, popcorn, and Coca-Cola—what some may jestingly label as "American staples."

Home-cooked meals are frequently replaced by food delivery services, with long queues of cars forming at drive-throughs near office buildings. Nonetheless, it is noteworthy, as my real estate agent once pointed out, that "when purchasing a new home, many prioritize having a pristine kitchen."

Ah, indeed! Recently, I have been observing a frenzied rush toward the curbside pickup phenomenon, where our American friends are graciously spared the taxing endeavor of strolling through a supermarket. Mon Dieu, it seems that anything capable of sparing them from breaking a sweat is hailed as a godsend!

And voilà! There are even applications that handle your grocery shopping for you. One can't help but ponder the direction in which America is heading with such innovations. I wouldn't be surprised if drive-through services, undoubtedly an American invention, begin serving escargot and croissants. Perhaps private chefs have become as commonplace as French baguettes in bakeries. Americans exhibit an unparalleled penchant for practicality, perpetually seeking ways to streamline their lives to the point of sheer elegance, n'est-ce pas?

CHAPTER 4

INHERITANCE AND FAMILY FRACTURE IN THE U.S

"Vos parents n'ont pas besoin de vos larmes quand ils vont mourir. Ils ont besoin de votre amour et de prendre soin d'eux de leur vivant." **French saying**.

(Your parents don't need your tears when they die. They need your love and care for them while they are alive.)

While attending the local YMCA in my town, I struck up friendships with several elderly gentlemen who frequented the place every morning for physical exercises and walks. I have always been inclined to engage in conversations with my elders, considering them living libraries of wisdom. With time, I ventured into their retirement homes and occasionally volunteered to help. Among them were John and Sue, dear friends from New England who had relocated to the South to escape the harsh winters.

During these interactions, I had the privilege of getting to know Vietnam veterans, individuals who inspired me profoundly. Each of them carried a unique life story, but there was a common thread. I couldn't help but notice that among these aging heroes were widowers and widows who had been forsaken by their own children.

Often, their offspring couldn't find the time for visits, or the geographical distance made regular contact challenging. In essence, many had cast aside their parents to focus on their own families, seemingly forgetting the sacrifices made by those who had given them everything: love and education.

As the years passed, I found myself attending numerous funerals, and witnessing the departures of these remarkable individuals from our world. Some were fortunate enough to have family members by their side during their final days, while others faced a lonelier journey.

This led me to contemplate whether the young generation of Americans, in their pursuit of self-interest, might have lost sight of a fundamental truth. Indeed, I encountered instances where it seemed all too common for self-centered children to reenter the lives of their aging parents solely when matters of inheritance were at stake.

From my experiences, I distilled four valuable lessons:

- Aging parents should never be abandoned simply because of their old age.

- Karma does not look kindly upon children who manipulate their elderly parents to seize their assets.

- If those elderly souls who departed while languishing in forgotten nursing homes could return to Earth for just one day, I suspect many would disinherit their ungrateful and heartless children.

- Growing old in the United States can be an arduous and trying ordeal.

At times, I ponder whether some grown children, in their eagerness to secure their parents' wealth and possessions, would hasten their demise if they could, or opt to send them to retirement homes with all possible haste.

CHAPTER 5

UNCHARGED BATTERIES: GERONCRACY IN THE US POLITICAL CLASS

"La vieillesse est une déchéance pour les hommes; il n'a pas de remède." **- GB**

(Old age is a decline for men; there is no cure.)

In the hallowed chambers of the U.S. Senate and the grandeur of the White House, a peculiar transformation is taking place. It's as if the annals of time have conspired to create an extraordinary spectacle - the American political elite, seemingly frozen in a realm untouched by the years. Mitch McConnell, the senior Senator from Kentucky, occasionally falters during his public addresses. The President of the United States himself, President Biden, has become a subject of concern due to a series of unfortunate falls. A good number of senators, most of them in their eighth decade of life, have now become reliant on wheelchairs. It begs the question: Who are the individuals choosing these elders to craft the laws that will influence the future?

The idea of revitalizing the political class seems to be an ever-receding mirage. These are the very leaders who tenaciously grasp onto power until the very end, despite the inevitable passage of time. The importance of recognizing when to step aside gracefully, making way for the younger generation, cannot be overstated. A failure to do so might appear self-indulgent and symbolize a decline in the United States that is difficult to ignore. The nation that I once knew, with its dynamic interplay of ideas, seems barely recognizable.

However, let it be known that the United States teems with youthful and vibrant politicians who hold the potential to breathe new life into the political landscape. They are the voices of tomorrow, brimming with fresh ideas and a fervor to shape a better future. Yet, the American political elite appears to grapple with the concept of gracefully passing the torch, and therein lies the conundrum.

The concerns regarding a President exhibiting signs of age-related cognitive decline should not be brushed aside lightly. How many more incidents must we bear witness to before recognizing that we may have reached a critical juncture? This morning, I awoke to the news that President Biden has aspirations for a second four-year term. While aspiration is commendable, there is a glaring divergence between one's aspirations and their practical capacity. It is a contrast underscored by the recurring falls and moments of vulnerability that have punctuated his tenure.

There is no need to conjure wild conspiracy theories or blame external forces like a KGB agent slipping a banana peel onto the President's path. These incidents are, quite simply, the unvarnished consequences of aging—a reality that transcends the boundaries of power and politics. The question that lingers is whether there is anyone in the President's inner circle providing sound counsel, perhaps suggesting the pragmatic use of a wheelchair given his proclivity for falls.

It is vital to remember that growing old is not synonymous with a dearth of wisdom. It is a phase of life that prompts us to reflect on the encroaching physical limitations that come with the passage of time.

CHAPTER 6

CHROMOSOMES AND CHUCKLES: A SCIENTIST'S TAKE ON U.S. RACIAL IDENTITY

"Il n'ya qu'une race humaine – scientifiquement, anthropologiquement. Le racism est une construction, une construction sociale...il a une function sociale, le racism." **T. Morrison**

(There is only one human race – scientifically and anthropologically. Racism is a construction, a social construction... it has a social function, racism.)

Upon my arrival in the United States, I was acutely aware of my Black heritage, yet I had never emphasized it as a defining aspect of my identity. This perspective was deeply rooted in my background as a scientist who rejects the notion of race as a biological concept. In my eyes, all human beings share three fundamental traits: their blood runs red, they possess 46 chromosomes, and their tears are colorless.

However, my journey in the United States took an intriguing turn when I encountered the practice of specifying one's race while completing forms for my social security card. The available options included Black or African American, White, American Indian or Alaska Native, Asian, Native Hawaiian or Other Pacific Islander, Hispanic or Latino, and Others.

It was in the U.S. that I began to grapple with questions surrounding my own racial identity, in stark contrast to France, where surveys based on race are prohibited. During my history classes in France, I learned that the countries bordering the Caucasus Mountains—such as Iran, Russia, Turkey, Armenia, and Georgia—were traditionally referred to as Caucasian.

This led me to ponder when and how white Americans, primarily of Anglo-Saxon origin, came to be classified as Caucasians. Despite the visual resemblance, the genetic intricacies remain elusive.

Furthermore, I questioned whether Americans were aware that "Hispanic" does not denote a specific race or ethnic group but rather a linguistic designation. Many individuals who identify as Hispanic can hail from a variety of racial backgrounds. I also found it peculiar that the vital registration system assigns a race or ethnicity to a newborn based on the mother's race, even though there is no scientific basis for such categorization.

This underscores the intricate nature of identity, one that defies simplistic categorizations. Isn't it a fascinating subject to explore? Oh, Mon Dieu!"

CHAPTER 7

SHADES OF LOVE: NAVIGATING INTERRACIAL MARRIAGES IN AMERICA

*"Si tu vas en guerre, prie une fois; si tu vas en mer, prie deux fois; si tu vas en mariage, prie trois fois.***" French Saying**

(If you go to war, pray once; if you go to sea, pray twice; if you are going to get married, pray three times.)

When I left France for the United States, I was acutely aware that as a Black man with ebony skin married to a white American woman, we would encounter unique challenges in a country where mixed couples aren't always celebrated. It's not the entire nation that's inherently racist, but certain institutions and individuals.

Despite this, we found profound happiness and serenity in our relationship. We chose to live in harmony, unaffected by the judgment of others. Our home is in the southern United States.

Our first encounter with racism took place at the home of a white American friend who had invited us to a barbecue and fireworks celebration on the 4th of July, marking U.S. Independence Day. As we sat on the balcony, a guest, a white woman in her fifties, greeted everyone and took a seat across from us. She locked eyes with us and declared, "I don't believe in mixing races. I disapprove of your relationship." In response, my wife firmly asserted that we didn't require her permission or approval to be together and happy. The exchange left a momentary silence, particularly since I was the only Black individual present.

Racism persists, whether in France or the United States, with prejudice always finding new avenues of expression. In regions once marked by segregation, mixed-race Black and white couples remain rare. Acceptance is more common in larger cities. Racism can be overt in conservative states and more veiled in liberal ones. It's disheartening to note that Alabama only repealed its laws against interracial marriages in 2000.

Love transcends color. In some states, such as Mississippi or Alabama, concerns about the changing demographics in the United States have led to apprehensions about becoming a minority. It's evident that the white population in the United States is having fewer children compared to other demographic groups.

It's disheartening to hear Donald Trump supporters opposing diversity, fearing the dilution of the Aryan race.

To navigate life in the United States as a Black man married to a white woman, one must fortify their moral resolve. It's not always smooth sailing, and there's no magical remedy for racism. I see racism as a conscious choice and ignorance in the face of diverse skin colors and cultures. Tolerance demands an open mind.

As long as Americans of different backgrounds remain within their respective bubbles, racial tensions will persist. Whether they like it or not, interracial unions represent the future of the United States and the world. These unions bring us closer together and foster harmonious coexistence.

I can't help but observe that Americans are preoccupied with race to an unusual degree. I reached my limit with racial issues during my first two years in this beautiful country.

Even within the Black community, I've been questioned numerous times about why I chose a white woman as my wife instead of a Black one. My response has remained consistent: it's not about race but personal preference. In life, some men prefer curvier women, while others prefer slimmer ones; some favor blondes, brunettes, Blacks, or Asians—everyone has their preferences.

In the United States, my beautiful daughters, who are biracial, are often labeled as Black. I find it amusing. How is it that white supremacists can impose this labeling on an entire nation while no other racial or ethnic group is categorized in this manner? It's baffling and absurd—a form of racism. In the United States, you are either Black or White; the concept of mixed ethnicity barely exists.

Unfortunately, whether in France or the United States, a mixed-race couple is still often referred to as a "mixed couple." Why not simply call it a "couple"? Long live diversity. C'est la vie!

CHAPTER 8

MISERY OF AMERICAN TEACHERS

"Celui qui sert bien ne doit pas craindre de demander son salaire." **French saying**

(He who serves well should not be afraid to ask for his wages.)

I was once married to a French teacher, and I must say that the issues teachers in France complain about pale in comparison to the monumental challenges faced by educators in the United States. The burdens placed on teachers here are immense: keeping up with ever-evolving technology, managing classroom behavior, fostering communication with parents, and the strenuous task of preparing and grading papers late into the night—all for a meager salary. It's disheartening to note that I don't know a single teacher who is genuinely content with their job or finds solace in their working conditions. In the United States, teaching is often a thankless endeavor, and many of the teachers I know regret their career choice. Who wouldn't contemplate a change in profession?

Being a teacher in the United States often feels like assuming two roles for a pittance: that of an educator and that of a babysitter. I'm certain that many individuals enter the teaching profession out of a true calling, but it's evident that the conditions of their professional life and the accompanying living standards don't align with their aspirations.

They find themselves forced to make choices between their health and sustenance, struggling to pay their bills because their income is so limited. How can this be happening in a country that claims to be the most powerful in the world? Recently, I was distressed to learn that American teachers are paid for only ten months a year, and during the two months of summer, which are meant to be a break, they must seek summer jobs simply to make ends meet. I find this utterly appalling.

Please forgive my somewhat pessimistic tone; it's human nature to first address what is amiss or what presents a challenge. Rarely do we open discussions when everything is proceeding smoothly. Undoubtedly, there are contented teachers who derive joy from the connections they forge with their students or find fulfillment in the creative process of lesson planning. However, the reality of being a teacher in the United States can be relentlessly nerve-wracking. On teacher workdays, it's intriguing to observe American mothers dealing with their own children. It's on those days that I truly appreciate and respect the work that teachers do in this country.

A teacher's primary role is to impart knowledge and essential skills to people of all ages, as without knowledge, life can become exceedingly challenging. While it's true that every profession deserves fair compensation, I firmly believe that teachers in the United States deserve salaries that are at least three times what they currently earn. One cannot put a price on the impact of managing the noise and behavior of children over the course of ten months.

CHAPTER 9

A FRENCH CAN NOT SURVIVE IN THE UNITED STATES

L'herbe est toujours plus verte ailleurs- **Alphonse Daudet**

(The grass is always green elsewhere)

I firmly believe that financial stability is a key factor in achieving happiness and security. This conviction led me to make the life-changing decision to immigrate to the United States, driven by a desire for self-reliance rather than a dependence on government assistance.

In France, the socialist system often unintentionally fosters dependency, especially for those of us with ambitious aspirations. It's as if the government provides croissants without teaching its citizens how to bake them in case of scarcity.

In contrast, the United States ties your financial situation closely to your ambitions and goals. The few fellow French individuals I knew who attempted to start a new life in the U.S. didn't last more than six months. Their main grievances were the demanding American work culture and the complexities of the healthcare system. Unfortunately, they made minimal effort to learn the English language, a critical factor for success in the United States. Here, proficiency in English and a commitment to education open doors to promising careers. Entrepreneurship thrives, with banks eager to support worthwhile ventures—a stark contrast to the situation in France.

If I were to rewind the clock, I would unquestionably choose the United States once again, where degrees and diligent hard work are handsomely rewarded.

As I embarked on my journey to the United States, I believed I had a firm grasp on the country, but I quickly came to realize that understanding this vast nation is a lifelong endeavor. The U.S. is a land of astonishing geography and rich history, where every corner holds unique stories waiting to be discovered.

In France, the socialist framework often permeates various aspects of life, and mediocrity can be a common theme. Whether it's renting a car or seeking police assistance in times of danger, one may find that things fall short of expectations. The nation appears structured in a way that caters primarily to the workforce, leaving little room for those with lofty aspirations and perhaps too much for those who contribute minimally and thrive on welfare. For ambitious individuals with dreams of wealth, it can be a challenging environment.

In the United States, labor unions have less influence in safeguarding employees against poor management or wrongful termination compared to France, where labor rights are highly esteemed, making it challenging to terminate an employee due to the prevalence of unions in every enterprise.

American society places significant emphasis on the value of hard work, a mindset instilled from a very young age. It's not uncommon to see young children setting up lemonade stands in American towns, reflecting an entrepreneurial spirit that begins in early childhood. The economic prowess of the United States is no mere coincidence.

The fear of economic instability often compels some Americans to take on multiple jobs. Conversely, in France, the "joie de vivre" often takes precedence over a strong work ethic. The 35-hour workweek law, while celebrated by some, is regarded by others as a preposterous and embarrassing regulation in human history.

French citizens sometimes demand a great deal from the government, and there's a tendency to apologize for working less in order to spend more time with family. However, the truth remains that working less often leads to earning less, making the resentment towards the wealthy somewhat irrational.

CHAPTER 10

RELATIONSHIP TO MONEY: FRENCH VS AMERICANS

"L'argent ne fait pas le bonheur, mais son absence fait le malheur." **French Saying**.

(Money does not bring happiness, but its absence brings unhappiness.)

Americans hold a deep-rooted affection for money, recognizing its intrinsic value and significance. The pursuit of wealth is often a challenging journey, and its absence can expose you to precarious circumstances.

Regardless of whether you are French or American, money serves as the engine that propels life forward. When you lack it, you might feel unnoticed, but with it, the world seems to bow at your feet. Money has a peculiar way of making you stand taller, even if you're not conventionally attractive.

For the affluent, admirers and opportunities abound; women pursue wealthy men, and men aspire to become gigolos or marry wealthy women. In the United States, wealth is often displayed openly, and there's no need to apologize for success. Wealthy Americans often find solace in charitable giving, provided their names and images are prominently displayed in local newsletters or on colossal screens during major sporting events.

My American friends don't hesitate to discuss the value of their cars, homes, or boats. In contrast, the French tend to be more reserved and cautious when it comes to discussions about money. Conversations about salaries remain largely taboo. In fact, the French readily share information about items or experiences that have cost them less money as if to deflect any suspicion of affluence.

One phenomenon that frequently leaves me astounded is the deep-seated resentment towards the wealthy that pervades French society. French billionaires, even those who are self-made, are sometimes referred to as vampires or parasites. It often appears easier to harbor jealousy than to muster the diligence required to acquire the house of one's dreams. In France, the wealthiest individual, Bernard Arnault, seems to hold a special place in the collective consciousness; the French adore hating him.

CHAPTER 11

THE TRAGIC HISTORY AND ONGOING STRUGGLES OF NATIVE AMERICANS IN THE UNITED STATES

"L'homme Blanc a invente les armes pour tuer, mais ces armes ne peuvent tuer la verite." **GB**

(The White man invented weapons to kill, but these weapons cannot kill the truth.)

The history of Native Americans is undoubtedly one of the most profound tragedies in human history, akin to the struggles faced by Black Americans. Wherever European settlers went, they left behind a litany of wrongdoing, resulting in immense suffering for the indigenous peoples of America. Native Americans endured massacres, exploitation, and the devastating impact of diseases brought by the newcomers.

To witness the contemporary lives of Native Americans, I embarked on journeys to states such as Dakota, Minnesota, Oklahoma, and Arizona. There, I had the opportunity to visit various tribes residing on different reservations. In hindsight, I must admit my naivety in assuming that today's Native Americans would closely resemble those from the conquered territories in the western United States.

I encountered tribes like the Apache and the Navajo, both of which had fascinated me during my younger years. Despite variations among reservations, commonalities emerged, notably the prevalence of casinos, alcohol, and drug-related issues.

Native American reservations have increasingly become tourist attractions, and I observed reservations with a more modern standard of living. In 2023, Native Americans accounted for an estimated 1.7 percent of the total U.S. population, primarily residing west of the Mississippi River. It's an unsettling reality that the Native American population was significantly reduced through both the actions of European settlers and the impact of diseases.

While they are referred to as "Natives" in the United States, they often prefer to be identified by their respective tribes. Regrettably, I've encountered very few Native Americans during my time here. Controversies surrounding their nomenclature persist, and the establishment of reservations as microstates within states, complete with their own legal systems, has occasionally led to friction with law enforcement.

For instance, in the state of Oklahoma, which I've visited several times, gambling is generally prohibited, yet casinos on reservations are legal. I frequented Choctaw casinos, which are part of a chain in Oklahoma owned and operated by the Choctaw Nation of Oklahoma.

I had the privilege of attending an annual Pow Wow, a North American Indian ceremony characterized by feasting, dancing, and singing. It was a vibrant and colorful event.

In conclusion, Native Americans are a minority of considerable rarity, constituting a smaller portion of the population compared to Black and Latino communities, estimated at 29% of the U.S. population.

There are days when I am profoundly disheartened when contemplating the lives of Native Americans. A few years ago, I considered visiting the Pine Ridge Indian Reservation in South Dakota, a place known for its extreme poverty and high crime rates. Unfortunately, I was strongly discouraged by a friend due to safety concerns for tourists. It's disheartening to learn that Pine Ridge is the poorest place in the United States, where people have a tragically short life expectancy due to alcoholism and drug addiction.

Necessities like drinking water and waste collection are lacking, and a staggering 85% of the population is unemployed. The profound irony lies in the fact that this suffering exists in the wealthiest country in the world.

It is devastating to realize that on 310 reservations in the United States, alcohol is technically "prohibited," yet a significant portion of the native population residing in these areas' grapples with alcoholism. I often wonder how individuals without employment can afford alcohol and drugs. Tragically, hand sanitizers and mouthwash have become lethal substances for some. Those who can afford alcohol often journey outside of reservations to make their purchases.

It is a cruel irony that those who were forcibly displaced from their land continue to be neglected by the U.S. government. In addition to these challenges, Native Americans continue to face racism from White Americans, reminiscent of the era of cowboys and settlers.

CHAPTER 12

THE UNSUNG HEROES OF AMERICAN AGRICULTURE: LATINOS AND STRUGGLE FOR A BETTER LIFE

"On ne peut aimer la pomme et detester le pommier." **French saying.**

(You can't love an apple and hate an apple tree.)

The United States is currently undergoing a significant transformation—a process often referred to as "Latinization"—that has become an everyday reality. Latinos play a pivotal role in ensuring that food reaches every table in the United States, from feeding President Joe Biden to the country's most economically disadvantaged citizens. Despite their invaluable contributions, many Latinos find themselves grappling to make ends meet each month. American farmers heavily rely on their labor, employing over 500,000 agricultural workers to plant, harvest, and package agricultural products.

In the United States, it's a common misconception to generalize all Latinos as "Mexicans" due to a lack of understanding, but the reality is far more nuanced. Latinos represent a diverse group, often stemming from a mixture of Native, white Spanish, or Portuguese heritage.

During election seasons, some political leaders resort to anti-immigration rhetoric to gain support among conservative voters. However, the truth paints a different picture. "Mestizos," as they are more accurately known, come to the U.S. in pursuit of improved living standards and job opportunities. They are willing to put in long hours, even involving their teenagers, to meet the needs of their families. Having faced poverty, they strive for financial security to ensure they never endure such hardship again.

Immigrants, frequently collectively labeled as "Mexicans," hail from various countries in South and Central America, all sharing a common goal of enhancing their quality of life. They are eager to work diligently and fill roles that many American citizens either do not wish to undertake or are less inclined to assume. The United States greatly depends on these committed workers.

Undocumented immigrants, a term used for those who entered the U.S. legally or illegally but have overstayed their visas, endure a challenging existence characterized by various injustices. They toil in low-wage jobs and often face exploitation. These individuals are the unsung heroes who labor tirelessly in the shadows—picking oranges in Florida's scorching heat, tending to crops in the Midwest's farming regions, engaging in house and road construction, and maintaining hotels.

What deeply concerns me is the indifference displayed by successive American administrations in failing to adopt a firm stance on regulating their immigration status. Many of these individuals are parents to children who are U.S. citizens and contribute to both state and federal taxes. This situation raises moral questions about how these people are treated and underscores the urgent need for change.

CHAPTER 13

THE COMPLEX LANDSCAPE OF ADOPTION IN THE UNITED STATES

"Pire que les mechants, il y a ceux qui font semblant d'etre bons." **French says**.

(**Worse than the bad people, there are those who pretend to be good.**)

Adopting or conceiving a child is a profound commitment that should never be taken lightly. Unlike adopting a pet, a child is not a commodity; they are unique individuals. The process of adoption, much like planning for a pregnancy, can come with unexpected surprises. Regardless of the circumstances, a child is a precious gift. While some aspects of the adoption culture in the U.S. may be surprising to foreign observers, it's crucial to remember that children are adopted out of love, and the love for an adopted or biological child should be no different.

Adoption regulations vary from state to state, making the United States an appealing destination for those with questionable motives in the adoption process. Shockingly, the U.S. has signed the International Convention on the Rights of the Child but has yet to ratify it.

Private adoption agencies in the United States are abundant, and at times, it seems their mission is to persuade young mothers without resources to give up their children for profit, with agency staff compensated on a commission basis. Regrettably, the best interests of the child often take a back seat. The lack of strong child protection laws allows for the exploitation of children, which is deeply troubling.

Discussing this issue can evoke a sense of despair. Online platforms, including Facebook groups and even Craigslist, occasionally feature advertisements offering adoption transactions with minimal oversight. Some websites encountered during research were deeply unsettling. The United States could greatly benefit from implementing a system that enforces stronger control and supervision.

This issue transcends ethical concerns and borders on human trafficking when children are treated as commodities. Moreover, the lack of scrutiny over prospective adoptive parents increases the risk of placing children in the wrong hands, potentially with individuals who pose a danger.

Understanding why certain countries, such as Russia, have prohibited Americans from adopting their children becomes evident. Reports of Russian children being abandoned by American adoptive parents underscore the need to shield children from a second abandonment. It's imperative to avoid generalizing between those who genuinely act in the best interests of the child and those who do not.

Another alarming phenomenon is what Americans call "rehoming," where adopted children are sought out for new homes. The reasons for such actions can be absurd, often citing the child's psychological issues while excelling academically. This amounts to the abandonment of a child adopted for selfish reasons and bears no distinction from those who abandon their pets.

This behavior is not surprising in a culture where returning merchandise to stores is common, but it is heart-wrenching when applied to children. Perhaps it is time to consider mandatory classes for future adoptive parents to prepare them for the challenges of raising a child, ensuring that the majority who adopt do so with the best intentions.

Respect is due to American families who adopt children with the genuine desire to provide them with a better life and unconditional love.

CHAPTER 14

THE ETHNIC EQUIVOCAL: DEMOCRATIC DECEPTIONS ON BLACK AMERICANS

"Les malades sont ingrats, ils ne pensent qu'au medecin que quand ils sont malades."

(The sick are ungrateful; they only think of the doctor when they are sick.)

When one first sets foot in the United States, a country celebrated for its diversity, you'll quickly discover that many minorities eagerly share their opinions about the political landscape. They often emphasize that the Democratic Party is the torchbearer of racial tolerance, while the Republicans, they insist, carry the heavy burden of harboring racists.

"Oh là," I thought as I embarked on my journey of making the U.S. my home. Yet, despite the shifts in political power, the core issues concerning the Black community appear to remain remarkably unchanged. It's as if the pendulum swings from left to right, but the heart of the matter remains immovable. Some argue that the Democrats quietly practice a form of veiled racism while the Republicans openly showcase their prejudices. The choice is left to you, the observer, to decide where your tolerance for different shades of racism lies. In the end, racism is racism, whether it's concealed or out in the open.

The Democrats, often seen as the saviors of racial equality, appear to take Black voters for granted. They summon the memory of Black issues with great fanfare during election season, making promises and commitments that inspire hope. But once the ballots are counted, and the cheers subside, they tend to vanish into the political ether, only to reemerge when the next electoral cycle looms. It's an eerie déjà vu, a cycle that prompts me to recall the famous saying, "The definition of insanity is repeating the same mistakes and expecting different outcomes." It's undeniable that racism remains deeply ingrained in the fabric of the United States. With a population of 41 million Black individuals, this community wields significant voting power that, if harnessed effectively, could be used to advance their cause.

What I found most perplexing is the Democrats' strategy to court my vote. They employ fear tactics, sounding alarms about Republican intentions to curtail abortion and contraception rights, impose Christian beliefs, and restrict transgender participation in school sports and access to medical transition treatments. They dispatch persuasive emissaries to my neighborhood, alluring messengers who ardently urge minorities to vote Democrat. Yet, once the election dust settles, these advocates vanish, only to reappear like clockwork when the next electoral cycle approaches. I find this political theatricality utterly absurd.

CHAPTER 15

REFLECTIONS ON TRUMP ERA: A JOURNEY THROUGH AMERICAN EVANGELICALISM

"Le fanatisme est une ver qui nait dans la pourriture religieuse." **GB**

(Fanatism is a worm that is born in religious rot.)

As an observer from France, my journey through American Evangelicalism during the Trump era has been eye-opening. If Jesus were to visit the United States, he would find himself facing significant challenges. This conclusion became apparent as I closely observed American Evangelical groups who ardently supported Donald Trump. To those unfamiliar with the context, it may seem perplexing, but Donald Trump, a shrewd political figure, grasped the mindset of White Christians who were uneasy about a non-white man in the White House. Their priorities revolved around faith, patriotism, firearms, and barbecue gatherings.

While Mr. Trump is far from resembling Jesus, he holds an almost divine status among these fervent believers. In France, such devotion would be labeled as a cult. What struck me most was the omnipresence of God in American political discourse. I attended several of Trump's rallies, not as an enthusiast but out of sheer curiosity. I even acquired a "Make America First" hat and a "Make America Great Again" T-shirt, only to discover that both items were manufactured in Taiwan.

My visits to President Trump's rallies exposed me to a wide spectrum of opinions. For instance, I overheard a gentleman claiming that Mitt Romney was a communist, a label seemingly unjustified for a former presidential candidate who was a lawyer and businessman. It seemed that Trump's supporters were quick to brand anyone who didn't support him as a "communist."

The casual use of labels like "communist" or "pedophile" and their entanglement with politics was perplexing. I was also disturbed by some shocking signs at these rallies, such as "Kill Biden," which seemed contrary to the Ten Commandments that prohibit taking a life unless I misunderstood the principles.

Trump's supporters came from diverse backgrounds, including born-again Christian groups who saw themselves as enlightened, while those who didn't share their faith were often viewed as dwelling in darkness. This spectrum of supporters included individuals from the LGBTQ+ community, Muslims, and even those associated with communism. The presence of "Christians for Trump" was prominent, identified by their distinctive T-shirts.

Among these groups, one could also find members of the American elite, distinguishable by their demeanor, speech, and business backgrounds. Engaging in conversation with them often raised suspicion. Surprisingly, it was easier to have an engaging conversation with an immigrant Uber driver than with these Americans who chose to remain within their own circles.

The America I once knew, where political disagreements could coexist with civility, seemed unrecognizable. Everything had become political, even the simplest of compliments, like praising a woman's dress. As for the potential candidacy of Trump in 2024, it appeared to be an act of sheer folly. The more he portrayed himself as a victim of political attacks, the more his supporters seemed willing to embrace him.

Many of his supporters firmly believed that the charges against their chosen candidate were nothing but concocted schemes by the judicial system. They held the belief that if one had nothing to hide, there was nothing to fear. Was President Trump sometimes a victim of his own outspokenness? I couldn't say for sure, but I did notice that whenever he spoke, controversy ensued on the opposing side, even though his odds remained high among Republicans.

During one rally, I struck up a conversation with a fervent Trump supporter who spoke of liberals fixating on Trump, diverting attention from the Hunter Biden affair and the alleged discovery of explicit material on his laptop. This news was entirely new to me, and I couldn't discern whether it was fact or fiction. For Trump's supporters, it was Hillary

Clinton's email scandal and Hunter Biden who deserved orange jumpsuits and imprisonment, as they were deemed worse than Donald Trump.

Attending Trump rallies felt like attending a one-man show for me. I was never disappointed, as there was always a medley of patriotism and nationalism. To quote one Trump enthusiast I overheard, "A mountain of suspicion is not worth an ounce of proof." God bless the United States!

CHAPTER 16

REFLECTIONS ON OBAMA'S PRESIDENCY AND CHALLENGE OF UNITY

"Les hommes imparfaits n'ont pas le droit de juger les autres hommes imparfaits."

Gandhi

(Imperfect men have no right to judge other imperfect men.)

When considering the legacy of Barack Obama, I often find myself approaching his presidency with care and thoughtfulness, avoiding the hasty judgments of the 44th President of the United States. This tendency for critique appears particularly prevalent among African Americans, with limited discussions on what Obama might have approached differently. It's essential to bear in mind that Obama's presidency aimed to serve all Americans, not solely the Black population, in the pursuit of fairness. Black Americans should reconsider their perspectives before passing judgment on Obama.

Despite being of mixed racial heritage, he faced numerous challenges during his time in office. Many of these challenges were presented by older white individuals who were determined to hinder his presidency, aiming to limit it to a single term through a policy of obstructionism.

Addressing the topic of race is never easy, but as a person of color, I find it more comfortable to discuss issues affecting Black communities than those of different racial backgrounds. America remains acutely aware of racial issues. The lasting impact of slavery on Black communities is undeniable, and it's crucial that we acknowledge this historical trauma while also working toward progress.

I may not be an ardent supporter of Obama; certain decisions in his administration's foreign policies left me feeling uneasy.

Leaders such as Dr. Martin Luther King Jr., Harry Belafonte, Malcolm X, John Lewis, and Jesse Jackson played their roles, but who will be the next generation of leaders?

The next generation of leaders will likely emerge from a foundation of unity, starting at the family level. This unity extends to Black American communities and addresses issues like intra-community violence, violence against Black women, and ensuring equal access to education. I find it increasingly challenging to accept excuses for why many young men seem averse to education. Education remains one of the most potent tools for combating racism and breaking free from the cycle of poverty.

It's an unfortunate reality that whites often possess a significant advantage from birth, setting them on an easier path to success. I acknowledge this inequity, and it's far from fair. However, not fighting back to redress these injustices is akin to self-sabotage.

While the Black Lives Matter movement vigorously addresses instances of Black individuals being killed in the United States, it is equally imperative for the movement to emphasize that Black-on-Black violence also claims lives. Violence, regardless of the perpetrator's race, is a tragic loss of life.

Chicago, Obama's hometown, is one of the most perilous cities where people of color often perpetrate violence against one another. What could Obama have done differently to curtail this? The answer remains a complex puzzle.

CHAPTER 17

RETIREMENT: NOT A REBOOT FOR BABYSITTING!

"Les coupables sont ceux qui profitent des autres." **GB**

(The culprits are those who take advantage of others.)

Retirement age opens a world of opportunities for travel and exploration, fulfilling lifelong dreams. However, it is disheartening to observe how many American adults lean on their parents to provide free childcare for their own children. The role of grandparents isn't primarily that of caregivers. If they choose to assist willingly, that's wonderful, but relying on them for childcare should not be an expectation when raising kids.

As a parent myself, I often witness weary grandparents straining to keep up with the boundless energy of young ones at public parks. It leaves me astounded when friends drop their children off at their parents' homes several times a week. New parents in the United States seem to embrace the idea of parenthood but struggle with the constraints it brings. Grandparents, like everyone else, have the right to enjoy vacations and evenings out.

I hold deep respect for and fully support grandparents who offer their help to young parents, especially recognizing that American mothers lack the extended maternity leave enjoyed by their French counterparts. However, my concern lies with grown adults who take advantage of their parents, regardless of their parents' own schedules. Grandparents should not be treated as nannies.

The relationship between grandparents and grandchildren is immensely valuable. The time spent together is a treasure trove of play and relaxation, strengthening the bond between generations. However, it is equally crucial for grandparents to prioritize their own well-being. Helping your children is commendable, but it shouldn't become a habit, as habit can erode relationships.

Living in the United States, I find myself pondering a significant societal issue. It seems that the new generation of parents often exhibits a sense of selfishness by expecting their parents, the grandparents, to shoulder a significant portion of the responsibility for their children's upbringing. Retirees deserve an active and fulfilling life after years of hard work. One cannot reasonably expect them to raise children all over again after the age of 60.

They have worked hard all their lives and, finally, are free from the obligations of their own children. The last thing they desire is to have dependent grandchildren.

To young Americans who plan on becoming parents, do not make the assumption that your parents must be your default babysitters. Some grandparents relocate to be closer to their children, leaving one to wonder whether it's by choice or out of fear of being labeled as inattentive grandparents.

For young couples seeking relaxation, a trip to the cinema, or a dinner date, planning and finding a babysitter should be the norm.

American grandparents, it's time to reclaim your retirement. You have already experienced the days of bottles, diapers, and baths. Retirement signifies the chance to travel, read, and engage in sports. Some grandparents may not have a natural affinity for infant care, and that's perfectly acceptable. Given the individualistic nature of American society, grandparents must learn to firmly decline requests to look after young children. It's not wrong; they, too, have every right to pursue their happiness.

CHAPTER 18

INEQUITIES IN THE AMERICAN JUSTICE SYSTEM: A TROUBLING REALITY

"Quand l'injustice surplombe la justice, il ya forcement une malveillance caracterisee de la part de l'esprit." **M. Khellaf**

(When injustice overwhelms justice, there is necessarily a characteristic malevolence on the part of the human spirit.)

The American justice system is often viewed as a business rather than a dispenser of true justice. Despite the presence of Bibles in every courtroom, their symbolic significance often falls short of preventing falsehoods and upholding integrity. In a legal landscape where factors such as race, social status, sexual orientation, and financial resources play defining roles, your fate may be determined long before your innocence or guilt is established. Many innocent individuals find themselves having to prove their innocence when there is no evidence against them, resulting in lasting trauma and emotional scars.

Even securing a favorable outcome in the initial arbitration does not guarantee freedom from legal entanglements. The possibility of losing on appeal exists, as those who lost their case one day can easily change lawyers with connections to judges the next. In such an environment, distinguishing right from wrong becomes an elusive pursuit. I personally experienced the challenge of requesting proof from a judge, which, in the context of an accusation, drew his ire.

Fortunately, I escaped formal charges due to the absence of a police report and physical evidence. I have never harmed a woman and never will. However, as a Black individual in the United States, one is often automatically viewed as a suspect.

Allegations of corruption among judges, police officers, and lawyers persist, while racial prejudice endures as an unyielding presence. Racial hatred is a sobering reality, and in the United States, being Black is often synonymous with danger and criminality. Prayers among Black and Latino individuals often involve avoiding a trial with a white male judge due to the perceived bias and prejudice they may face.

The accountability of judges for errors in the pursuit of justice remains elusive. Incompetent judges seem to be shielded for life, leaving countless lives shattered in their wake due to erroneous judgments. The atmosphere in American courts can be disheartening, with white male judges often projecting an air of superiority protected by armed police officers.

It's disheartening to discover that judges cannot be held liable during or after their tenure. The label "destroyers of lives" seems apt for some judges despite the presence of fair and non-racist judges who are, unfortunately, in the minority. The overall picture suggests a pervasive lack of honesty within the system.

One can't help but imagine that many innocent individuals are convicted and languish in jails, some even meeting execution. The disparities in the treatment of Black people before white male judges are particularly striking. The composition of the jury further determines the fate of a person of color in a trial.

Even one's own lawyers may disappoint, with their motivations sometimes guided by financial considerations, often seeking to gauge the size of one's retirement account before deciding how vigorously they will advocate on one's behalf. Some lawyers who have personal connections with judges may manipulate the system to secure a judge of their choice.

In certain instances, within the United States, lawyers may gain access to police reports pertaining to speeding violations. Consequently, individuals who commit such violations frequently receive solicitation letters from attorneys eager to represent them in exchange for a fee. These legal professionals often successfully "negotiate" a reduction of the speeding ticket to a lesser offense, such as a parking ticket.

While this practice might be labeled as corruption in some developed nations, in the United States, it is not commonly categorized as such. Oh, mon dieu!

What unfolds in American courts can, at times, appear more like a scripted performance, a circus where lawyers pre-determine the outcomes of cases. This deeply troubling reality underscores the need for systemic reform and a renewed commitment to ensure justice is truly blind and impartial.

CHAPTER 19

AMERICAN COLLEGE STUDENTS BELIEVE IN THE POWER OF DRINKING.

"Ne pas dire non ne veut pas dire oui." **GB**

(Not saying no doesn't mean yes.)

It's a stark reality: as I ventured into American college life, I found myself confronted by a set of issues that encompassed alcohol, tobacco, and narcotics, with a particular emphasis on the problems related to alcohol. American colleges have gained notoriety for their drinking culture, and my journey into this culture was both eye-opening and, at times, deeply concerning.

According to the National Sexual Violence Resource Center, distressing statistics reveal that one in five women and one in 16 men fall victim to sexual assault during their college years. I couldn't help but notice the strong connection between alcohol and sexual assault, often leading to severe consequences.

Compounding the issue is the legal drinking age in the United States, set at 21 years. Consequently, it's not uncommon to witness students attempting to purchase alcohol using fake IDs at local convenience stores near their campuses.

The lack of restraint when it comes to alcohol consumption is a cause for concern, with certain universities even earning the reputation of being "party schools."

Whether celebrating a victory or commiserating a loss during sporting events, students consistently find a reason to indulge in alcohol. Tragically, this circumstance can lead to grave consequences, including cases of sexual assault due to a lack of consent. In many cases, alcohol becomes the silent perpetrator, effectively serving as a date rape drug at student parties.

Even brilliant students have found themselves accused of rape after falling into this perilous mix of alcohol and sex. The truth is, when I engaged in such risky behavior, I had to accept the possibility of adverse outcomes, and I learned that the blame should not be solely laid on alcohol.

One contributing factor to this alarming trend is the absence of moral and civic education courses in the United States. This deficiency, in my opinion, has led to the prevalent attitude that "anything goes." It appears that the role of teaching responsibility and understanding the consequences of one's actions has been shifted from parents to the police and hospitals. Many parents fail to educate their children about the challenges they may face on college campuses.

Meeting up in another student's apartment, especially when unsure of one's feelings for the person, may not be a wise decision. This is not a one-size-fits-all perspective, and there may be varying opinions on the matter. However, I've observed that American society often unjustly places blame on the victim when a sexual assault occurs at the perpetrator's residence.

Many students fail to understand that even in intimate situations, every individual has the right to say no. This situation is reminiscent of a small-town mayor in Mississippi who, in 1964, attempted to justify the assassination of three civil rights workers, Chaney, Goodman, and Schwerner, by stating, "They knew it was risky to come down here, so it was their own fault." This attitude reflects a dangerous tendency to shift blame onto the victim. Some may argue that, on American college campuses, the prevalence of alcohol consumption makes it akin to a realm where the influence of negative forces, often likened to "Satan," is pervasive.

CHAPTER 20

A HARROWING ENCOUNTER WITH THE AMERICAN HEALTHCARE SYSTEM

"Qui est en bonne sante aux Etats-Unis est riche sans le savoir." **GB**

(He who is in good health in the United States is rich without knowing it.)

Three months after I arrived in the United States, I fell ill with the flu, and what unfolded was nothing short of bewildering. Rushed to the emergency room, I received prompt treatment and was later discharged. However, what took me by surprise, even though I had health insurance, was a hefty $400 deductible that awaited me.

At that moment, I couldn't help but wonder if there had been some mistake, perhaps an extra zero mistakenly added to that $40. Nevertheless, I found myself with no choice but to pay the $400. As a newcomer to this country, one of the earliest pieces of advice I received from Americans was to promptly settle any debts or risk tarnishing one's credit rating.

As time passed, I made a friend who happened to be a French surgeon. He had made the bold decision to sell his clinic in France and immigrate to the United States. Eight months into his American journey, he fell seriously ill and required emergency surgery for appendicitis. Shockingly, the cost of this operation added up to nearly $20,000, all for just one night in the hospital. To add insult to injury, the hospital charged a staggering $10 for a simple bottle of water as his wife anxiously stood by his side.

My understanding of the deficiencies in the American healthcare system deepened rapidly. How could such exorbitant bills be justified? It became glaringly obvious to me that even those of us considered "lucky" to have health coverage were not entirely safe.

My heart went out to the countless Americans with meager incomes, possessing only basic health coverage, who were forced into agonizing decisions. They had to choose between preserving their eyesight or sacrificing their dental health, among other impossible choices. This was no way to survive in a country that once promised the American Dream but now often felt more like an American nightmare.

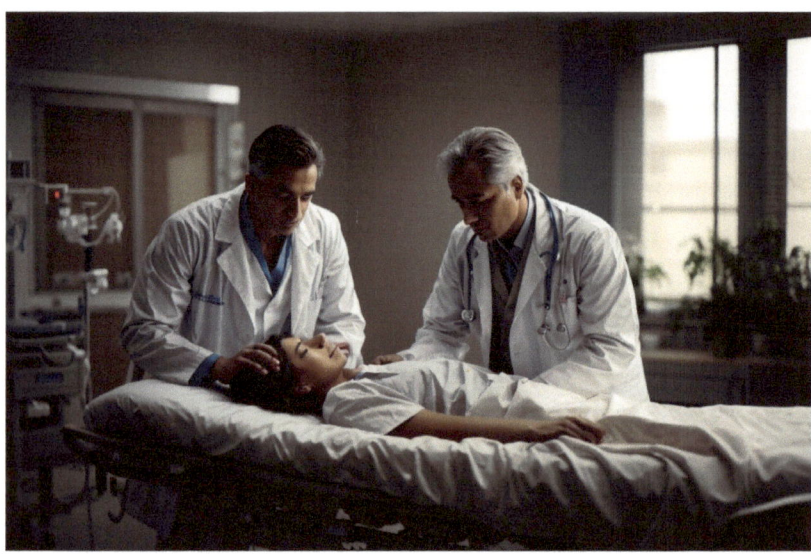

I quickly realized that in the U.S., if you didn't adhere to a perfectly healthy lifestyle, you were essentially teetering on the edge of a precipice. It made me wonder how the world's largest economy could prioritize its military arsenal over the well-being of its citizens. I found myself searching for answers, unsure of which saint to pray to. The national motto, "In God We Trust," took on new significance. How could this be when God seemed to be everywhere, even in hospitals? Incidentally, hospitals were predominantly managed by private companies focused on profit. I often pondered whether American doctors pursued medicine out of a sense of vocation or merely to amass wealth. The explanations I heard often cited student loans and other financial burdens, but the stark reality was that the healthcare system appeared to be an orchestrated collusion between hospitals and insurance companies.

Paying your health insurance premiums month after month did not guarantee that your coverage would be honored when a serious illness reared its head. Unfortunately, I came to realize that the American populace was somewhat naive and extraordinarily averse to the term "universal healthcare."

The drumbeat of Republican propaganda painted it as a form of socialism. In the end, the disease didn't care whether you were a liberal or a conservative; it was an equal-opportunity adversary, leading to the same destination for everyone—the cemetery. It began to feel as though the Hippocratic Oath was more of a "hypocrite's oath" in the United States. Faced with it all, one could only hope that America would find a way to bless itself with a more equitable and compassionate healthcare system.

CHAPTER 21

BLACK-ON-BLACK RACISM IN THE UNITED STATES

"Le racisme est une manière de deleguer a l'autre le degout qu'on a de soi-meme." **R. Sabatier**

(Racism is a way of delegating to others the disgust we have for ourselves.)

Allow me to share my personal reflections, filled with observations from my life as a person of color living in the United States. It's important to emphasize that, in my perspective, individuals of all races, whether they are white, black, Asian, or belonging to any other ethnicity, are individuals of color.

Unfortunately, human ignorance knows no limits; it surpasses racial boundaries and manifests in various forms. Sometimes, it feels as if racism permeates the very air we breathe, evident in the glances exchanged in restaurants, particularly when I, a black individual, am in the company of a white couple.

Gender seems irrelevant, and for a black male, the experience can be even more challenging. It's a phenomenon that persists whether you are in New York, Boston, Los Angeles, Atlanta, or even Adair, Iowa.

Now, if you are a black individual from Africa or the Caribbean living in the United States, you may encounter two distinct manifestations of racism. Firstly, there is the troubling "black-on-black" racism, as some black Americans seemingly choose to overlook their African origins. Those individuals often fail to earn my respect, a lesson my grandmother, Elizabeth, instilled in me during my formative years: 'Do not do unto others what you would not want them to do to you.'

Another regrettable manifestation of racism is the 'black versus others' dynamic. I have come to believe that everyone possesses some degree of racial bias, whether conscious or unconscious. Consequently, I have learned to exercise caution in forming judgments. The world is vast, and it's unwise to judge an entire race based on the actions of certain individuals."

CHAPTER 22

NAVIGATING LOVE, RELATIONSHIPS, AND PARENTHOOD IN AMERICA

"Il ne faudrait pas que celui qui vient de donner son sperme s'en lave les mains." **C. Boutin**

(The person who has just donated sperm should not wash their hands of it.)

In the United States, regardless of your economic status, safeguarding your sexual health and future is crucial. Always use condoms when engaging in sexual activity, whether you're married or single. A divorce can be a costly affair, and the expenses multiply when children are involved.

In some communities, certain men find themselves labeled as 'baby daddies,' a term referring to men who father children with multiple women. The consequences of not exercising control over one's sexuality and leaping into relationships without caution can be substantial.

I don't want to sound overly pessimistic, but it often appears that marriage offers limited benefits to men in the United States. The American justice system, while equitable in many cases, is not always so. Therefore, one should exercise great care when choosing a life partner, regardless of gender.

Prioritizing the well-being of your children is imperative, even when you may be upset with their mother. What I have observed is that some women, when it suits them, opt for abortion with the consent of their partners, especially if the partner is financially strained. Yet, when they see an opportunity for financial gain, they choose to keep the child and seek child support. This can result in the heavy burden of child support, potential custody disputes, and various manipulations. Unfortunately, there are individuals in the United States who seem to lack love or compassion for their own children.

In the United States, it often appears that the legal system leans in favor of the mother, even if she has a substantial income. Judges may sometimes be perceived as biased against fathers. It's truly bewildering! Despite these challenges, it's crucial to do right by your child, no matter the circumstances.

So, gentlemen, exercise caution in your choices, be mindful of the potential consequences, and avoid fathering children without careful consideration. Choose your partners wisely and always ensure you are protected during intimate encounters. Ah, the complexities of life as a man! C'est la vie!

CHAPTER 23

SAN FRANCISCO: WHERE LOVE TAKES CENTER STAGE

"L'amour est le meilleur analgesique contre la haine." **GB**

(Love is the best painkiller against hate.)

I once believed that Pigalle, a neighborhood in Paris, was the undisputed gay capital of the world. Still, my perspective shifted when I set foot in San Francisco. This vibrant city revealed itself as a global giant in the realm of gay and lesbian communities. It was my inaugural visit to the city, and what I encountered was nothing short of beautiful—a place where tolerance openly thrived on its streets and in its parks.

The myth that gays and lesbians are anything but normal dissolved as I witnessed same-sex couples joyfully playing with their children. It leaves one pondering: What could possibly be wrong when a loving, capable couple is ready to embrace the role of adoptive parents, offering shelter and nurturing to children in need? Homophobia, akin to the persistent specter of racism, may persist, but we must learn to disregard hatred, for there exists no cure for such venomous sentiments.

Homosexuality is not a recent phenomenon; it has been part of our world for centuries. Therefore, the refusal to recognize same-sex marriage and adoption of children strikes me as illogical. It's a misconception that only heterosexual couples hold a monopoly on raising children well. After all, how many individuals raised by heterosexual parents turn out to be less than stellar human beings?

A child raised by a gay couple may experience a different upbringing compared to what they might have encountered in a heterosexual household, but "different" doesn't necessarily translate to "bad." It takes an open mind and a heart brimming with tolerance to recognize the sincerity and goodwill that the gay community brings to the table.

In San Francisco, I had the pleasure of witnessing the beauty of mixed couples from diverse races, and I thought to myself, "Well done!" Love, it seems, is the ultimate antidote to the venom of hatred and intolerance, and it's a delightful twist in the comedy of life that we should all embrace.

CHAPTER 24

UNVEILING THE ARTS OF AMERICAN PROFANITY: A CULTURAL EXPLORATION

"Bite, c'est un gros mot, meme si c'est une petite." **Coluche**

(Dick is a bad word, even if it's a small one.)

When we learn a language, we tend to pick up swear words quickly. American bluntness is an integral part of the cultural landscape. The FCC (Federal Communications Commission), an American institution created to uphold moral standards by preventing profanity on television, often seems powerless in the face of this culture. Television channels have adeptly discovered ways to skirt sanctions. American TV channels have mastered the art of evasion, adding beeps after swear words, even the notorious "F-word."

Evasion is prevalent in everyday language: "Fuck" occasionally morphs into "Fork," and "Bullshit" subtly transforms into "Bullshirt." To my French ears, it sounded no different. What frequently amuses me is the level of paranoia and hypocrisy on American television. Swearing is a national pastime in the United States; it's ubiquitous—in parks, at work, within families, and in movies.

Americans swear as naturally as they breathe, whether they're happy or not. The "beeps" can't contain it! I've come to realize that it's deeply ingrained in the culture. Whether young or old, there's always room for the F-word in a sentence, injecting a touch of humor into conversations. Children learn to swear by their parents or friends. If profanity were a form of wealth, everyone in the U.S. would be rich.

I recall then-Senator Joe Biden, known for his unfiltered speech. My initial encounters with certain words were puzzling, like "Ass," which meant an idiot, and then "being an asshole" left me utterly bewildered. The very words that should not be uttered on television were the most commonly heard expressions in everyday life. If Google could categorize people based on the frequency of their use, I would certainly be renowned. I, too, was eager to watch George Carlin's sketch, "Seven Dirty Words," to enhance my English. These words continue to captivate me due to their diverse usage in American English, often conveying various meanings. Oh, la la!

"Cunt," "Cocksucker," "Shit," "Fuck," "Tits," "Piss," "Screwing," the "B" word, the "F" word, "Hell yeah," and "Motherfuckers." Oh my! I pondered what the Puritans might have wrought upon these people. Even today, numerous taboos continue to astound me. However, "WTF" remains the phrase that never fails to bring a smile to my face because American English without this expression is like a bird without wings. I remember "Keep my wife's name out of your mouth," proclaimed by Will Smith after a confrontation with comedian Chris Rock at the Oscars; it served as yet another confirmation of the prevalence of swearing in America.

CHAPTER 25

AMERICANS AND THE EVOLVING NOTIONS OF RELATIONSHIPS AND INFIDELITY

"Le libertinage c'est aimer au pluriel tout en restant singlier." **French saying**

(Libertinism is loving in the plural while remaining singular.)

I'm aware that adultery is considered a criminal offense in fifteen states in the United States. According to statistics from the American Association for Marriage and Family Therapy, 15% of married women and 25% of married men have had extramarital affairs, underscoring the societal disapproval of infidelity.

In a world filled with modern temptations, such as dating apps on smartphones, it becomes more understandable why some couples choose to explore open relationships. As time passes, it's not uncommon for individuals to encounter challenges in maintaining a satisfying and long-term sexual connection. The prevalence of sexless marriages in the United States is a stark reality. For some, leading somewhat parallel lives can rekindle sexual desires, though I acknowledge that this perspective may not align with certain religious beliefs.

After spending a significant number of years together, it's not surprising for a couple to witness changes in their approach to sexuality. Each person holds their unique vision of a partnership, and perhaps it's healthier for all parties involved to openly agree on their terms instead of resorting to deceit. While this relationship model may not be universally suitable, there are individuals who do not view their spouse being intimate with another person as an act of betrayal.

The proliferation of marriage dating sites in the United States highlights the underlying unease within many marriages. In such cases, one may question why someone would choose to remain in a relationship marked by infidelity rather than embrace singlehood. Personally, I find infidelity unforgivable, regardless of the rationale behind it.

Ménage à trois exists in France, but it is not exclusive to the French. Friends who engage in it share the same vision of love and partnership.

In an open and consensual relationship, where both partners willingly agree, individuals can pursue what they desire, potentially fostering a healthier connection. It's important to remember that exclusivity does not resonate with everyone. While Americans tend to idealize the concept of a couple, the reality often reflects individualism. While religious values are highly regarded, it's essential to recognize that America is not a theocracy.

I often find amusement in the complexity attributed to sexual advice offered by American couples' therapists, as they sometimes overcomplicate matters.

Ultimately, pragmatism should prevail. If a consensually open relationship brings happiness to a couple, that's what truly matters. It's worth noting that there are men who may feel threatened by sex toys but struggle to satisfy their partners in bed. In such cases, sex therapists and solutions like the "blue pill" are available to assist couples. C'est la vie!

CHAPTER 26

THE SECOND AMENDMENT DILEMMA: A PARENT'S PERSPECTIVE ON SCHOOL SHOOTINGS

"Face à un problème, il n'y a pas 36 solutions: il faut lui trouver une solution." **Edith Cresson**

(Faced with a problem, there are not 36 solutions: you must find a solution.)

Since my arrival in the United States, I've frequently contemplated the deep-seated attachment of Americans to their Second Amendment. The enduring fervor for it continues to baffle me. The tragedy of school shootings impacts us all, whether we are parents or not. As a father, my heart races with anxiety when I receive a text alert notifying me that my children's school is on lockdown due to an unidentified individual roaming its halls. Last year, bullets were found in the boys' bathroom; oh, mon Dieu!

In a nation where firearms seem to outnumber the total population, I'm perpetually wrestling with questions about how to best prevent, curtail, or manage the heart-wrenching spate of school shootings. Firearms, in many ways, resemble an inescapable curse. They circulate, both legally and illicitly, throughout the entire expanse of the United States. If these weapons are as accessible as croissants in a bakery, controlling them becomes an almost insurmountable challenge.

It's evident that mere prayers won't suffice to quell the relentless epidemic of mass shootings. Unfortunately, the prospect of a miraculous solution remains elusive, and mass killings may continue to haunt the United States. Efforts to abolish the Second Amendment are fraught with the potential to incite insurrection, adding complexity to the issue.

As a parent, I've grown accustomed to discussing guns with my children in much the same way we discuss the topic of sex. It's disheartening that children in the United States can't experience the innocence of growing up without the specter of gun violence. We educate our children on how to respond to fires and earthquakes, but when it comes to shootings, we are rendered helpless.

The debate surrounding firearms inevitably resurfaces after each school massacre. Questions arise, such as whether teachers should be armed. Personally, I can't envision sending my children to school in the care of armed educators, given the inherent risks associated with such a strategy. There's always the unsettling possibility that a teacher might lose control and unleash chaos. Arming teachers to counteract shootings feels akin to an arsonist trying to extinguish a fire.

In a heart-wrenching conversation with my high school-aged daughter, she posed a chilling question: "What should I do if I hide and the shooter finds me?" I found myself without an adequate response.

If the gun lobbies maintain their immense influence, it appears unlikely that meaningful change will occur in the United States. Moreover, the lack of comprehensive state support for mental health issues further exacerbates the situation. Amid these pressing concerns, I can't help but reflect on the complex and multifaceted issue of the Second Amendment and its profound impact on our society, particularly as a parent. Oh, mon Dieu!

CHAPTER 27

THE QUANDARY OF PAYING ON THE FIRST DATE: NAVIGATING AMERICAN PERSPECTIVES.

*"La galanterie c'est l'art de mettre une femme en valeur.***" French saying**

(Gallantry is the art of highlighting a woman.)

Over the years, I have found American women's attitudes toward who should foot the bill on a first date to be rather perplexing. I find it peculiar—there's nothing gallant about it. When a man covers the expenses of a first date, it doesn't necessarily imply that he's purchasing your company or your conscience. I can't recall anyone going bankrupt for picking up the dinner tab. If things don't work out well, c'est la vie!

Sometimes, there's no need to overanalyze things. Life can be simple. Our acts of kindness aren't solely driven by the desire for intimacy. This idea of feeling obligated to sleep with someone or to be indebted after dinner is a product of a materialistic society, in my view—a society that believes in a strict "tit for tat" mentality. In cases of incompatibility, it can be challenging to transition to intimacy after settling the bill.

True elegance lies in not insisting on covering everything. I have met women who don't appreciate feeling beholden.

People in America often seem to have lost the ability to appreciate nuances. If a man chooses to be chivalrous, it's entirely his prerogative. Likewise, if a woman opts to split the bill, it's also her choice. However, it's crucial to remember that one should never feel obligated to reward a man with physical intimacy in exchange for a mere $30 lunch. Such a notion is simply absurd!

CHAPTER 28

AMERICAN HUSBANDING: BALANCING HOUSEHOLD ROLES FOR A HARMONIOUS MARRIAGE

"Mon mari dit qu'il veut passer ses vacances dans un endroit ou il n'est jamais alle. J'ai repondu: et pourquoi pas la cuisine? "**Nan Tucket**

(My husband says he wants to spend his vacation somewhere he's never been. I answered: and why not the kitchen?)

I advocate for domestic harmony in the United States. Recently, I had a conversation with a gentleman who claimed that, in his religion, house cleaning was not a task for men; it was predominantly a woman's responsibility. I couldn't help but wonder if he was referring to some obscure belief system.

What strikes me—as my American married female friends often affirm—is that once a man has a wife at home, he seemingly forgets how to perform household chores. Yet, when he was single, he managed laundry, house cleaning, and dishes just fine.

Personally, I believe that it's essential to maintain the same level of affection and pursuit in a relationship after marriage, a point that many men tend to overlook. In my own marriage, I had a list of things that I used to do prior to marriage that I made sure to continue. A man who marries a woman for no specific reason may inadvertently be seeking a live-in maid rather than a partner.

To my fellow American men, I'd like to emphasize that if your wife stays at home to raise your children, do not underestimate the difficulty of her job. Being a stay-at-home mom is an exhausting endeavor; between cleaning, laundry, and tending to children who demand attention every five minutes, it can be overwhelmingly demanding.

I've heard countless testimonials from mothers, especially those with younger children and homemakers, who find themselves juggling various responsibilities throughout the day. American stay-at-home moms are, at times, unfairly characterized as lazy by some husbands. In reality, their roles encompass being a mother, homemaker, and wife—equivalent to three or four jobs. They do it all without receiving a paycheck.

Dear American husbands, it's imperative to appreciate and value the work your wives do at home. It's ten times more exhausting than working in an office. If you desire a happy marriage, occasionally helping with household tasks such as vacuuming or operating the washing machine can make a significant difference to your wife. A man's participation also encompasses maintaining the heating system, mowing the lawn, vehicle upkeep, fixing or cleaning the car, addressing plumbing issues, and handling trash disposal.

I came across an article discussing a study on Australian women, which suggested that a woman's libido can decline when household chores are disproportionately divided between partners. This study isn't limited to Australia and can be applied to French and American couples as well. It may also offer insights into the high divorce rate in the United States.

A man who mows the lawn or changes a light bulb is not diminished in any way. Life is an investment, as my grandmother often reminded me. The more a man participates in household tasks, the less resentment there will be, ultimately contributing to a healthier, more satisfying, intimate life. When we're less fatigued, we can channel our energy toward our intimate relationships.

Marriage should offer a safe and nurturing space for love. Unfortunately, for many women, it can turn into a confining experience of exploitation rather than a realm of genuine affection and partnership.

CHAPTER 29

UNSEEN INJUSTICES: RACISM IN THE U.S. AND FRANCE

"Le racisme n'a pas de frontieres." **French saying**.

(Racism has no frontiers.)

In the United States, thousands of individuals' stories echo the tragedy of George Floyd. They are like anonymous soldiers who fell silently, with no discrete videos to capture their brutal deaths. Reflecting on how the French media covered the George Floyd incident, I am struck by the naivety and hypocrisy within the French press. French journalists seem eager to create headlines and documentaries about everything that goes wrong in the United States, from crimes in Chicago to the latest incidents of police violence against Black individuals.

Regrettably, the same French media often lack the courage to denounce injustices against minorities in France, such as the case of Adama Traoré, a young Black Frenchman who tragically died in police custody.

This raises a fundamental question: Is it better to live in France as a Black individual or in the United States? It's a topic I frequently debate with my friends. Racism in France is expressed in a uniquely subtle yet aggressive manner. In the name of preserving France's image, the country often denies the Black French identity, whether in representation, media, cuisine, or culture. It's only when Black individuals achieve excellence in sports or cinema, such as Omar Sy, the actor from "Lupin," that France proudly acknowledges their achievements.

A multicultural and multicolored French society, as exemplified by the victorious national football team, is celebrated. However, being a non-white Frenchman still entails the exhausting task of explaining one's origins, even if one was born in France.

It becomes evident that the issues faced by Black communities in both the United States and France share striking similarities. Challenges related to employment, education, housing, and police violence are universal concerns. But what have Black people done to offend the good God to deserve such treatment anywhere in the world?

The scourge of anti-Black racism is not limited to the United States; it is a global issue. Racism is not merely the absence of love; it is the presence of hatred.

CHAPTER 30

TABOOS AND MISCONCEPTIONS: A GLIMPSE INTO AMERICAN SEXUALITY

"La pruderie c'est l'hypocrisie de la pudeur." **French saying**

(Prudery is the hypocrisy of modesty.)

The United States, often seen as a puritanical nation, raised eyebrows when it elected Donald Trump, a figure with a history laden with peculiar tales about women.

This juxtaposition challenges the notion of American puritanism, revealing a complex relationship between Americans and their understanding of sex. It seems that sex is a subject that captivates and mystifies Americans, almost as if they believe God is listening to their every conversation—an intriguing aspect of American culture.

Americans, it appears, could benefit from a more relaxed perspective on sex. It's not uncommon to feel like a sex educator when engaging with an American partner. The use of terms like "foreplay" in American sexual discourse can inadvertently suggest that penetration is the main focus of the sexual experience, which is far from the truth. The importance of touch and other forms of intimacy is often overlooked.

Sex out of a sense of "marital duty" is not genuinely enjoyable; it becomes a constraint. Many Americans equate sex exclusively with penile-vaginal penetration, a notion that is limiting and inaccurate. Sexual intercourse encompasses a wide range of experiences beyond this single act. Oh, la la!

Certain television series, like "American Pie" and "Sex and the City," may be seen as provocative, yet the sacredness associated with sex in the United States often leads to a paradox. The emphasis on performance and an erect penis as a sign of sexual desire can be misleading, as stress and nervousness can affect male arousal. Understanding the sensitivity of a woman's body and the significance of mutual satisfaction should be more widely taught.

Misconceptions about menstruation persist, with some believing it renders a woman "untouchable." The notion that a large penis is a prerequisite for satisfying a woman is unfounded. Claims that masturbation and pornography reduce intellectual capacity leave us questioning their origin and validity.

Sexuality extends beyond the physical act, encompassing emotional and psychological dimensions. While parenting lessons are offered in some high schools, there is a strong focus on abstinence, overshadowing the importance of teaching practical knowledge like condom use and contraceptive methods. The high rate of teenage pregnancies in the United States suggests a need for comprehensive sex education with a primary emphasis on prevention.

In the realm of intimate relationships, the responsibility for achieving sexual satisfaction should not be one-sided. Men should be facilitators, but a woman's ability to achieve orgasm lies in her own hands, both literally and figuratively. It's a shared journey, not solely the responsibility of one partner.

The inclusion of parenting lessons in high school raises questions about individual choices, as not everyone aspires to be a parent. In the realm of politics, the cautious avoidance of topics related to sex is often observed, reflecting a fear of losing support from certain voter demographics. This extends to a reluctance to use terms like "condoms" and a tendency to sidestep issues such as teen pregnancies.

Indeed, American sexuality remains a topic shrouded in taboo and sometimes puzzling misconceptions.

CHAPTER 31

VERBAL FIREWORKS: POLITICAL INSULTS IN THE AGE OF TRUMP

"L'insulte est souvent l'argument final de celui qui ne trouve plus rien a dire." **French saying.**

(The insult is often the final argument of someone who can't find anything more to say.)

In today's political climate, engaging in discussions can feel like navigating a minefield, potentially impacting one's mental and physical well-being. Political extremism, present on both the right and the left, has deeply permeated various facets of American society.

Criticizing a president is a fundamental exercise of freedom of speech and a cornerstone of democracy. However, it prompts the question: how far should this criticism go? Every American president will inevitably have their critics. What truly perturbs me is the glaring lack of courtesy and respect in exchanges between Americans with differing political views.

This leads one to ponder whether the United States has lost sight of its core values or whether it ever truly upheld them.

The case of Donald Trump represents a unique chapter in this nation's history, given his often incoherent behavior and a notable lack of self-control in his interactions with others. Furthermore, he serves as a lucrative subject for the American media and global onlookers. By critiquing him through his words and actions, the press inadvertently lays the groundwork for his potential return to the White House in 2024, fueled by his consistently high approval ratings among his supporters.

Now, let's delve into the disheartening yet somewhat absurd exchanges between pro- and anti-Trump factions. Brace yourself; the realms of nonsense and human ignorance appear boundless.

CHAPTER 32

WHAT LIBERALS SAY ABOUT PRESIDENT TRUMP AND HIS SUPPORTERS

President Macron of France visiting President Trump at the White House

"Macron + Donald = MacDonald" **Anonymous**

"Never in the history of the United States has any President been so hated; every day in the press, he is a caricature." **Anonymous**

"Trump supporters are incurably mentally ill." **Collin C.**

"According to a scientific survey, Pro-Trump people have a lower IQ than rats." **Anonymous**

"Putin and Trump friend? Not really. One off to jail and the other off to hell." **Anonymous**

"Pro-Trump supporters are unvaccinated assholes." **Anonymous**

"Trump fanatics trust Putin much more than they do under the democratic reign of Joe Biden." **Anonymous**

"Fostering a coup is called being a sore loser." **Marcus**

"The only one who thinks Trump was a great President is Donald Trump himself. His supporters think so because Trump said so." **Anonymous**

"Trump supporters really don't know what to make up anymore." **Anonymous**

"Make America Greedy Again." **Johnny**.

"The White Evangelicals Christians are hypocrites of the first order. They are no better than the Taliban." **Anonymous**

"The vast majority of the US despise Donald Trump; he has destroyed our country and our image worldwide." **Anonymous**

"I regard Donald Trump as having very poor moral standards and being incompetent as a President." **Anonymous**

"Donald Trump is a pathological liar, a bully, and an ignorant. We are embarrassed." **Cindy P.**

"I decided to move to Europe as long Donald Trump is President. I refused to live in a country run by a wannabe dictator." **Peter C.**

"My husband and I hate Donald Trump with a passion. He's a crook." **Mary T.**

"Can you believe that? Trump called Canada a national security threat." **John M.**

CHAPTER 33

WHAT DONALD TRUMP FANS SAY...

"Obama could have prevented 911."

"At President Trump's inauguration, people came from all over the world...Florida, Arizona, Arkansas." **KJ**

"If all the people in the world had a President like Trump, it would be happiness for humanity." **Corinne B.**

"President Trump is a visionary; he predicted that Germany would depend on Russia." **N.M.**

"I saw President Trump win on TV, then I was told he lost. I know he won. So, it's a stolen election." **Bob T.**

"I am going to say a prayer every day that Donald Trump wins in 2024." David B.

"Obama destroyed the United States." **John M.**

"The defeat of Donald Trump began the fall of Western civilization." **E. B**

"Joe Biden is a communist." **Anonymous**

"Kennedy and Donald Trump are the best Presidents in the history of the United States." **Jonathan**.

"Are you blind or stupid? Trump is the best presidential candidate. Prepare for major depression in 2024." **Paul**

"Trump is the greatest job creator God has ever created." **Mathew D.**

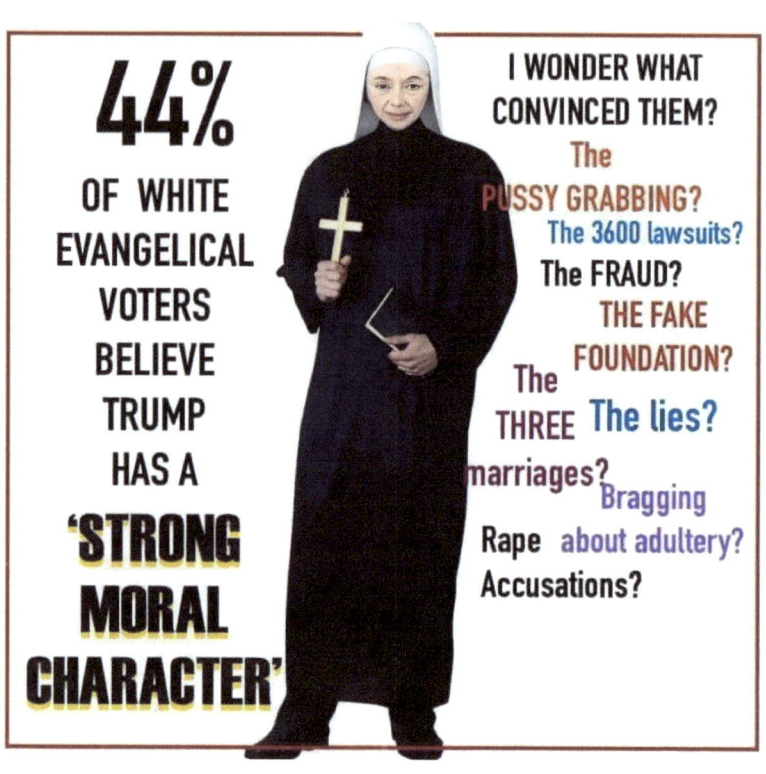

44%
OF WHITE
EVANGELICAL
VOTERS
BELIEVE
TRUMP
HAS A
'STRONG
MORAL
CHARACTER'

I WONDER WHAT CONVINCED THEM?
The PUSSY GRABBING?
The 3600 lawsuits?
The FRAUD?
THE FAKE FOUNDATION?
The THREE marriages?
The lies?
Bragging about adultery?
Rape Accusations?

"God made the right choice to choose Donald Trump over Hillary Clinton, a billionaire over a satanist liar. Monica Lewinski was right." **Linda R.**

"The Democrats' strategy has always been to demonize Donald Trump." **David**.

"Life under Trump was much better. My paycheck gave me more freedom than under the present communist regime. "**Daniel P.**

"Donald Trump is sent by a miracle to defend our constitution and our freedom." **Monica B.**

"Trump, a President who wins with all the media against him. When he was a Hollywood liberal, the media loved him. Whether we like him or not. His self-confidence and his determination inspire." **John**

"To this day, I wonder where the doctors who said Trump was crazy went?" **Jean P**.

CHAPTER 34

THE PROUD BOYS PUZZLE: A PERSONAL JOURNEY

"Le fanatisme est l'apanage des ignorants." **French saying**.

(Fanaticism is the prerogative of the ignorant.)

The Proud Boys, distinct from communists, have positioned themselves as a modern-day counterpart to the Ku Klux Klan, priding themselves on their "patriotism" and "courage." Picture them as the American equivalent of France's far-right enthusiasts, but armed.

What amuses me is that some Proud Boys are captivated by a conspiracy theory about White Americans facing genocide. Frankly, I believe that for some White Americans, the fear of losing privilege outweighs the fear of actual extermination. Loving your country is admirable, but it shouldn't translate into hatred for others.

The Proud Boys firmly believe that no country can outshine the United States. It reminds me of a man who swears he has the most attractive physique but has never ventured into a men's locker room. True appreciation of your country comes when you explore others.

One of the rare moments I've seen Donald Trump not uttering something outrageous on television, which is indeed an oddity, was when he addressed the Proud Boys, his ardent supporters. Honestly, I thought it was a scripted comedy.

Have you noticed the Fred Perry polo shirts adorned by the Proud Boys? These have associations with far-right skinheads in both the U.S. and the U.K. It sends shivers down your spine.

In my fictional world, imagine if the same polo manufacturer produced identical rainbow polo shirts - the Proud Boys versus the Pride Boys, an epic showdown in the United States!

The group claims to champion freedom of speech but isn't hesitant to resort to violence against those with opposing views. Frankly, there's no rhyme or reason to it!

American men have always intrigued me; they seem like children trapped in adult bodies. There's a perpetual air of aggression. As a martial arts black belt, I've always viewed aggression as a sign of weakness. It has nothing to do with masculinity. Trust me, when you're self-assured and recognize your potential, there's no need for loud proclamations. A tiger doesn't announce its identity.

I've always held the belief that using verbal or physical violence against those with differing opinions is nothing short of fascism. Hence, every group in the United States, be it liberal or conservative, can be accused of such tendencies. I have witnessed violence even in movements like Black Lives Matter.

When I've encountered anti-immigrant and Trump supporters, I have often asked if they know the exact number of illegal immigrants residing in the U.S., to which I've received the consistent answer: "A lot." But "a lot" is hardly a number. This is the peril of using propaganda for political gain.

I find it rather foolish to be born in the United States and harbor anti-immigrant sentiments in a country built by immigrants. In a nutshell, I find folly dispersed across all continents.

Enrique Tarrio, leader of the Proud Boys, strikes me as a particularly intriguing and peculiar character. How did he, an Afro-Cuban and Afro-Latino, manage to lead a predominantly white extremist group? The contradictions are simply mind-boggling!

CHAPTER 35

REFLECTIONS ON THE TRUMP ERA: MEDIA, OPINIONS, AND THE AMERICAN DEMOCRACY

"Meme si tu n'aimes pas le lion, reconnait quand meme qu'il est le roi de la jungle."

(Even though you don't like the Lion, recognize that he is the king of the jungle.)

The ongoing saga playing out in the courts feels like it's scripted straight from the pages of a Hollywood production. It's a mix of media propaganda and the intricate workings of justice, and I've even heard some of his ardent supporters claim that the crimes attributed to him are nothing but fabricated accusations. They maintain that the only way to prevent him from running for president again would be through drastic measures—a testament to the deep divide in opinions about the man. Some fervently argue that he is not a despicable figure and that he was never a poor president.

Within the realm of the French press, there seems to be an unexplained tendency to revile and disparage Donald Trump. It's a quirk of French culture, a penchant for criticizing successful businessmen. Personally, I don't count myself among President Trump's cheerleaders, but I strive to retain objectivity. Mr. Trump is an enigmatic and intriguing character; you either like him or you don't. However, my opinion doesn't prevent me from finding him captivating. His detractors emphasize certain aspects of his personality and actions, leading me to question the American media's trustworthiness.

In the United States, media outlets rarely, if ever, remain neutral. Oddly, this works in Mr. Trump's favor; the more liberal media criticizes him, the more support he seems to garner. It's an interesting phenomenon. Truth, even if uncomfortable for some of my liberal and democratic friends, is of utmost importance. We all have a tendency to view things from our own perspectives. I do not look down upon individuals with differing opinions. The United States is a remarkable democracy where listening to all voices is imperative. If Mr. Trump believes in securing American borders based on certain assumptions about Mexicans and Muslims, it's his right to do so. Many, including myself, may hold contrasting views, but attempting to silence him is not the answer. My stance is not influenced by any group; it revolves solely around my aversion to prejudice and racism.

One cannot become the President of the United States by chance; regardless of what anyone asserts, his legacy is indelible in the annals of American history. After his passing, this man will look back from heaven, realizing that he lived an extraordinary life on Earth. Accusations of racism and misogyny have become an integral part of his history and that of the United States. It's worth noting that my position is not aligned with either Trump or Biden, for I believe that in this complex political landscape, understanding diverse perspectives is vital.

CHAPTER 36

THE AMERICAN EPIDEMIC: OPIOIDS, PROFITS, AND CONSEQUENCES

"La dependence est bien l'un des resorts les plus puissants et les plus efficacies de l'activite humaine." **Albert Memmi**

(Dependency is indeed one of the most powerful and efficient resorts of human activity.)

Drug use in the United States has grown into an epidemic of staggering proportions. At the core of this crisis is the reckless prescription of opioids, where financial interests often overshadow reason. Having had the privilege of visiting various states in the U.S., I witnessed the devastating impact of drug abuse, particularly among the younger generation.

The complicity of some doctors in prescribing dangerous drugs that harm society is nothing short of a tragedy. Instead of channeling trillions of dollars into warfare and the production of government weapons of mass destruction, it is high time that Americans address the grave issues festering within their own borders due to this drug epidemic.

Opioids are wreaking havoc in communities across the country, with OxyContin being one of the most frequently prescribed opioids. This potent painkiller is handed out by American doctors as if they were distributing candy.

Reading an article from the CDC (Centers for Disease Control and Prevention), I was taken aback to learn that a staggering 80% of the world's OxyContin production is consumed by Americans. It raises the question: Is there anything Americans don't consume in excess? Perhaps vegetables.

I recall learning in school that the marketing of drugs is authorized by the FDA if scientific experts, free from conflicts of interest, demonstrate that the drugs are not dangerous. However, I cannot help but notice the glaring failure of the American government to address this tragic issue, which does not receive the attention it deserves.

I want to make it clear that I cherish my life in the United States, and my intention is not to denigrate this beautiful country. However, it's evident that here, everything can be sacrificed for the sake of profit. The principles of free enterprise have led individuals to legally establish businesses that sell anything, even if it has the potential to ruin lives. This includes items ranging from sex toys and food to guns and medicines, as long as they can be sold and generate profit. The lack of strict regulation is concerning.

The question that arises is whether this is the American dream in question or a consequence of capitalism. How can we explain that pharmaceutical companies peddle both the remedy and the poison simultaneously? Companies like Purdue Pharma are akin to drug dealers, merchants of death, and perhaps even worse, as people believe they are seeking treatment when they are, in fact, buying their own demise.

American cities at night often resemble ghost towns, with the night belonging to drug addicts and chronically depressed individuals. It begs the question: Has America lost its humanity? The prevalence of extreme individualism stands in stark contrast to the backdrop of deep religiosity, with churches lining almost every street in America.

Throughout my time living in the United States, this nation has grappled with the drug problem, and it seems to have consistently lost this battle. Is there state corruption at play, influenced by major pharmaceutical companies? Who are these doctors prescribing powerful and highly addictive painkillers instead of less addictive alternatives like ibuprofen? With over 130 people succumbing to drug overdoses daily, primarily from prescribed opioids, the government should be targeting the pharmaceutical lobbies. It's evident that, in the United States, the focus tends to be on treating the effects of drugs rather than addressing the root causes.

CHAPTER 37

FRENCH EXPATRIATES IN THE UNITED STATES: A TALE OF TWO COMMUNITIES

Qui se ressemble, s'assemble." **French saying**

(Birds of the same feather flock together.)

Across the United States, a vibrant French community thrives, creating a diverse tapestry across this vast nation. The French, renowned for their sociable nature, tend to gravitate toward their fellow compatriots, often engaging in conversations primarily in their native language. Many of them choose to reside in neighborhoods populated by other French expatriates and enroll their children in French high schools.

Within the United States, two distinct categories of French expatriates emerge. The first category consists of those who have called the U.S. home for over two decades, often having married Americans. Many within this group hold strong criticisms of their country of origin, occasionally viewing the French political and economic systems as flawed and labeling their fellow countrymen as indolent. Ironically, it's often toward the end of their lives that some of them contemplate returning to France.

The second category comprises French newcomers who exhibit a lesser inclination to assimilate into American society. They tend to be highly critical and frequently express grievances about various aspects of their American experience. Unlike their counterparts in France, they lack the privilege of going on strike if the quality of their bread or cheese falls short of expectations. Even after several years of residing in the U.S., their command of the English language typically remains at a middle school level.

Interestingly, immigrants in France often face similar criticism due to language barriers and are also accused of failing to fully integrate into French society, highlighting the universal challenges of expatriate life.

CHAPTER 38

WEALTH DISPARITIES AND HOMELESSNESS IN THE UNITED STATES: A PARADOX OF PLENTY

"Un Americain sans travail est une personne morte." **GB**

(An American without a job is a dead person.)

In the United States, success is frequently measured by financial prosperity, where one's wallet size becomes a yardstick for their accomplishments. It's both puzzling and disheartening to witness the wealthy occupying lavish homes while others face the harsh realities of life on the unforgiving streets, struggling to find a place to call home.

This stark contrast is evident from the sprawling streets of Los Angeles to the sunny shores of Florida. America cannot conceal this troubling disparity. I've even heard some individuals attempt to explain homelessness as a chosen lifestyle, a conscious decision on how to live. Personally, I find it hard to believe that anyone would willingly opt for the bottom rung of the social ladder.

Many of those who endure life on the streets are likely veterans who once dutifully served their country. Others are diligent, hardworking individuals who, through the cruel twists of fate, lost everything overnight, leaving them destitute, without a roof over their heads, and no funds to their name. This is an unacceptable reality.

Herein lies a perplexing paradox. In a nation teeming with homelessness, we see the existence of colossal, opulent houses. The United States, at times, becomes a land of extremes and contradictions. While I understand that owning a substantial home can often symbolize a certain status, the stark incongruity of having some of the most extravagant houses coexisting with people who have no place to call home is both disconcerting and perplexing.

CHAPTER 39

LOVE BEYOND BORDERS: AMERICAN MEN AND UKRAINIAN WOMEN DEBUNK STEREOTYPES

"Si l'amour rend aveugle, les problemes rendent la vue." **French saying**

(If love makes you blind, problems make you see.)

In recent times, I have observed American men in relationships with Ukrainian women. I've often pondered why Ukrainian women sometimes receive an unfair reputation in the U.S. when they're involved with Americans. Unjustly or not, they are occasionally suspected of seeking a green card or financial gain.

This situation reminds me of the unfair generalization that labels all Muslims as terrorists. Such sweeping stereotypes are plainly unjust. When Western men, including Americans, show interest in Eastern European women, they may occasionally disparage Western women to justify their choice of a younger, blond Ukrainian partner. I've heard comments such as, "Western women are extremely abusive, cold, and materialistic," with feminism often being blamed.

The truth is people are people, regardless of their origins. There are no guarantees in life, and marriage is a matter of chance, whether you marry an American or a Ukrainian. Men should avoid the naïve assumption that life will be significantly easier just because their partner hails from somewhere other than the West.

When it comes to loyalty, nationality makes no difference. You can just as easily marry a Ukrainian woman who might be unfaithful as you could an American woman.

Americans are often perceived as affluent compared to the rest of the world, and it might be challenging for a Ukrainian woman to believe that there are financially struggling men in the U.S.

I apologize for this generalization, but I've witnessed an example close to home. A cousin of mine studies in Odesa, Ukraine, and he now carries many regrets. His ex-wife didn't embrace modern views of marriage; she strongly believed that a man should be the sole breadwinner in the family, while her role was to cook, clean, maintain her attractiveness, and provide intimacy to her husband.

In situations where one spouse doesn't contribute financially, you can predict the outcome unless you are exceptionally wealthy. Here's another lesson I've learned: when money became tight, she decided to get a part-time job, but the money she earned was hers alone, while her husband's income was for both. After their divorce, she wasted no time in finding someone wealthier.

It's crucial to remember that my cousin's ex-wife doesn't represent all Ukrainian women. My point here is that in any culture, you will find both good and not-so-good individuals. French men may be disappointed with French women, American men with American women, and Canadian men with Canadian women. The list is endless.

For those men exploring Ukrainian dating sites, I urge you to engage your intellect and learn about their culture and traditions before committing. If you are grappling with personal issues, it's wise to address them before embarking on a relationship to avoid further complications.

CHAPTER 40

AMERICAN DREAMS AND FINANCIAL REALITIES: NAVIGATING THE CONSUMERIST LIFESTYLE

"Une vision sans action n'est qu'un reve." **French saying.**

(Vision without action is just a dream.)

When I inquire about the life goals of the average American, I frequently encounter two common responses: "I aspire to be my own boss" or "I'm striving for financial freedom." I often find myself admiring the audacity of the American dream, even as it appears paradoxical when compared to daily life.

Many Americans face challenges in achieving financial independence due to a lack of discipline and patience. They are enticed by the allure of quick gains through day trading, seeking short-term solutions.

Consumerism in the United States is akin to a deeply ingrained religion. Parents often pass down their spending habits to their children, perpetuating a cycle from one generation to the next. Thrifty individuals are a rare find among my friends. When I visit their homes, I discover discount coupons aplenty, and their houses seem like treasure troves, containing everything from canned goods and bread to rice and pasta.

Despite this, many rarely cook because they are lured by weekend sales. When Americans accumulate an excess of belongings, they struggle to let go, relegating them to garages, obscure corners of their homes, or storage units. I sometimes ponder the reasons for such hoarding tendencies, but the explanations are often evasive, with the term "sentimental" frequently cropping up. It's almost as if over-purchasing has become a compulsive condition. I am no psychologist, but I suspect a connection.

American banks profit immensely each year from overdraft fees and other banking charges, collectively amassing billions of dollars prior to the COVID-19 pandemic. Yet, it's a rarity to hear an American discuss consulting with a financial advisor to learn about better saving and spending practices. They typically seek financial advice only when borrowing money.

I have a friend married to a bank's financial advisor, who often humorously remarks on her husband's spending habits. This situation humorously illustrates that even experts in the field sometimes overlook their own financial matters, like the cobbler's children having no shoes.

American society relentlessly encourages spending, with advertisements bombarding individuals, whether they are on trains, highways, or watching television. Escaping this constant barrage is a formidable challenge. It's akin to a weed smoker trying to quit while constantly being enticed to smoke more; it creates a self-perpetuating cycle that's difficult to break.

Perhaps one potential solution for Americans is to leave their credit cards at home when going out, opting for cash to gain better control over their spending.

Having traveled extensively in various countries, I've observed that the United States is a place where students often live like employees. There's surprisingly little difference in spending habits between workers and students. Both groups frequently rely on their credit cards or, in the case of students, their parents' money or borrowed funds.

Once, I asked a therapist friend whether excessive spending could be considered an addiction, and he affirmed my suspicion. Interestingly, women seem to be more willing to seek psychological assistance for this issue than men. It's my belief that many American men have resistance to therapists, as consulting one may require confronting and admitting psychological issues, which can be perceived as a threat to their sense of strength and ego.

In relationships, it's not uncommon for couples to find themselves locked in disputes over spending habits, with one partner trying to persuade the other to curb their expenditure. However, attempting to curb an addiction can be as challenging as asking a liberal to become a conservative in the United States. It's a daunting endeavor.

The omnipresence of scratch games, gambling, and casinos, even at gas stations, reveals the pervasive vulnerability of Americans. It's as if they're caught in a perpetual trap, contending with an enduring temptation.

CHAPTER 41

ABORTION RIGHTS = DIABOLIC DECISION

"La femme n'est victime d'aucune mysterieuse fatalite: Il ne faut pas conclure que ses ovaires la condamnent a vivre eternellement a genoux." **Simone de Beauvoir**

(The woman is not the victim of any mysterious fatality: We must not conclude that her ovaries condemn her to live eternally on her knees.)

The recent decision by the United States Supreme Court has left me deeply concerned. I never thought I would witness a threat to abortion rights in my lifetime, and I find myself in disbelief.

The Supreme Court's decision to entrust the regulation of abortion to individual state legislators across the 50 states means that certain states, primarily in the South, may choose to prohibit and even criminalize abortion. I find this situation scandalous because, in my view, legislators, often predominantly men, should not have authority over this matter. Abortion is fundamentally a question of individual rights.

This decision is a significant setback for all women—a blow that resonates with fathers like me who have daughters in America. I believe in supporting my children in their decisions, and I want to make it clear that my concern extends beyond my gender.

To the male members of the American Supreme Court who supported this restriction, I say, shame on you! Men can never truly understand the intricacies of a woman's body, and while I may personally have reservations about abortion, I respect a woman's right to choose whether to carry a pregnancy to term.

I recall a situation from years ago when a friend faced an unplanned pregnancy and contemplated an abortion. Her partner was not ready to become a father, and her family pressured her to terminate the pregnancy. She sought my opinion, and despite the challenges, she decided to continue with the pregnancy. Her partner left her during this time, but today, she and her 11-year-old daughter share a close bond. Having a child outside of marriage is not a disgrace; it is a gift from God—c'est la vie!

I live in the United States, and I am cognizant of the challenges that mothers face, from expensive daycare to the complexities of life. Some may argue that people should abstain from sexual relations, but that is not a practical or realistic solution. Forcing a woman to carry a pregnancy to term in a country where women are not adequately supported is ludicrous. We must uphold the right to choose and the right not to choose. The United States was founded on democratic principles, not theocratic ones.

May God bless America as we navigate this critical issue with compassion and respect for individual autonomy.

THE AMAZING FACTS ABOUT THE UNITED STATES / THE QUIRKY AMERICAN FACTS- AS EXPLORED BY A CURIOUS FRENCHMAN

- ❖ Ah, February 14: Valentine's Day, or as they say, "National Condom Day" in the U.S.
- ❖ Mon Dieu, Bless America!
- ❖ Sacre bleu! The United States is known for exporting more sperm than anyone else in the world!
- ❖ For joining the American army, it is essential to have all ten toes intact. Mais oui!
- ❖ Mon Dieu! They used to forbid Black-White marriages in some U.S. states from 1776 to 1967.
- ❖ Zut alors! 100 divorces every hour in the United States. C'est incroyable!
- ❖ "In God We Trust" became their official motto only in 1956. That's quite late, n'est ce pas?
- ❖ Trump and Reagan were the only divorced candidates who became presidents in U.S. history. Ooh la la!
- ❖ It's estimated that 60% of Americans order food to take away chaque semaine. They love their takeout!
- ❖ About 20 million Americans live in mobile homes. Ah, c'est la vie- whether you sleep in a chateau or mobile, c'est le sommeil that matters!
- ❖ Mes amis, did you know that the largest group of people with expired visas in the U.S. are les Canadiens? It seems they are incognito in a predominantly white country!
- ❖ Only four minutes to become a presidential candidate in the U.S. Oh la la! If only I were born in the USA, I'd try my luck, too!
- ❖ George Washington, the man with 189 namesakes, including 8 streams, 1 state, 33 counties, 10 lakes, 9 colleges, and 121 cities and towns. That's a lot of Georges!

- Les femmes in the U.S. own 30% of all businesses. C'est fantastique, especially compared to France!
- Malheureusement: a young black person is 5 times more likely to be killed by the police compared to a young white person. Mon Dieu, the U.S. still has beaucoup de travail à faire.
- The number of prisoners in the world is around 11 million, and a quarter of them are in the United States. C'est incroyable, non?
- Sacrebleu! Around 40% of American babies are born from common-law unions. ça va surement choquer les traditionalistes!
- In case of pregnancy by rape, in 31 states of the U.S., a rapist can legally sue for custody of the child. C'est vraiment étrange, n'est pas?
- In 2022, the U.S. was the third most visited country in the world, after France and Spain, with 50.5 million visitors. Vive le tourisme!
- Despite English being the most spoken language, the U.S. doesn't have an official national language. C'est surprenant, n'est ce pas?
- Mon Dieu! "Made in China," American flags are banned in the U.S. army. Zut alors!
- GPS, mes amis, is the property of the American government. They guide us even in our dreams!
- In Montana, you will find three times more cows than humans. Sacre cows!
- Nearly 250,000 Americans meet their end each year due to medical errors. Le stress and profit above safety, c'est incroyable!
- Cigarette smoke, it seems, claims around 50,000 lives chaque annee in the U.S. Smoking is not tres chic!
- It is legal for a minor to smoke in the U.S., but buying cigarettes? Non, non, non!
- Un, deux, trois! One in three Americans might be considering a diet, n'est ce pas?
- West Virginia, with its forests along the Appalachians, is a picturesque state. But "Big Ugly"? Mes amis, I had to Google it to believe my ears!

- ❖ The United States boasts the world's most valuable passport. Superpower, super passport!
- ❖ An American citizen's daily dose is 600 sodas per year. C'est magnifique, but don't forget water!
- ❖ The U.S. is a land of opportunities but not paid maternity leave for working women. C'est dommage!
- ❖ Bananas, the favorite fruit of America. Tres bien, nature's fast food!
- ❖ One in seven Americans, mes amis, are card collectors, but not the trading kind they call them "consumption drugs."
- ❖ More TVs in the U.S. than people in the United Kingdom. Perhaps they are watching each other!
- ❖ Fewer married folks, more singles in the United States. Marriage, c'est pas pour tout le monde!
- ❖ One in eight Americans, perhaps, has flipped burgers at McDonald's. A McJob for all, it seems!

www.ingramcontent.com/pod-product-compliance
Lightning Source LLC
Chambersburg PA
CBHW040846120626
46547CB00001R/42